The World of DC

M000200573

The first sustained study of the DC Comics Multiverse, this book explores its history, meanings, and lasting influence. The multiverse is a unique exercise in world-building: a series of parallel and interactive worlds with a cohesive cosmology, developed by various creators over more than 50 years.

In examining DC's unique worlds and characters, the book illustrates the expansive potential of a multiverse, full of characters, histories, geographies, religions, ethnographies, and more, and allowing for expressions of legacy, multiplicity, and play that have defined much of DC Comics' output. It shows how a multiverse can be a vital, energizing part of any imaginary world, and argues that students and creators of such worlds would do well to explore the implications and complexities of this world-building technique.

Andrew J. Friedenthal has crafted a groundbreaking, engaging, and thoughtful examination of the multiverse, of interest to scholars and enthusiasts of not just comics studies, but also the fields of media studies and imaginary world studies.

Andrew J. Friedenthal is an independent scholar, writer, and critic living in Austin, Texas. His previous publications include *Retcon Games: Retroactive Continuity and the Hyperlinking of America*, chapters in the collections *Crossing Boundaries in Graphic Narrative: Essays on Forms* and *Transgressive Tales: Queering the Grimms*, and articles in the scholarly journals *ImageTexT* and *The Journal of Comics & Culture*. Additionally, he is a regular theater critic for the *Austin American-Statesman* and pop culture columnist for the online magazine *Sightlines*.

Imaginary Worlds

Each volume in the Imaginary Worlds book series addresses a specific imaginary world, examining it in the light of a variety of approaches, including transmedial studies, world design, narrative, genre, form, content, authorship and reception, and its context within the imaginary world tradition. Each volume covers a historically significant imaginary world (in all its manifestations), and collectively the books in this series will produce an intimate examination of the imaginary world tradition, through the concrete details of the famous and influential worlds that have set the course and changed the direction of subcreation as an activity.

The World of Mister Rogers' Neighborhood
Mark J.P. Wolf

The World of The Walking Dead
Matthew Freeman

The World of DC Comics
Andrew J. Friedenthal

The World of DC Comics

Andrew J. Friedenthal

Routledge
Taylor & Francis Group
New York London

First published 2019
by Routledge
605 Third Avenue, New York, NY 10017

and by Routledge
2 Park Square, Milton Park, Abingdon, Oxon, OX14 4RN

First issued in paperback 2021

Routledge is an imprint of the Taylor & Francis Group, an informa business

Library of Congress Cataloging-in-Publication Data
Names: Friedenthal, Andrew J., author.
Title: The world of DC comics / Andrew J. Friedenthal.
Description: New York, NY : Routledge, 2019. | Series: Imaginary worlds |
    Includes bibliographical references and index.
Identifiers: LCCN 2018060074 (print) | LCCN 2018060209 (ebook) |
    ISBN 9781351248952 (master eBook) | ISBN 9780815370574
    (hardback : alk. paper)
Subjects: LCSH: DC Comics, Inc. | Comic books, strips, etc.—United
    States—History and criticism. | Imaginary places in literature.
Classification: LCC PN6725 (ebook) | LCC PN6725 .F75 2019 (print) |
    DDC 741.5/973—dc23
LC record available at https://lccn.loc.gov/2018060074

ISBN 13: 978-1-03-209270-6 (pbk)
ISBN 13: 978-0-8153-7057-4 (hbk)

Typeset in Times New Roman
by Swales & Willis Ltd, Exeter, Devon, UK

Dedicated to Kaley

(the immutable core of my own private multiverse)

to Aunt Marylin

(whose wisdom is only matched by her humor and kindness)

and to John & Stephanie

(who, somewhere out there, are having a good time)

Contents

Acknowledgments

No scholarly work, even a relatively short one such as this, exists in a void. Without the following people, this book would not have been possible.

I was both surprised and honored when Mark J.P. Wolf asked me to be a part of this series. His *Building Imaginary Worlds: The Theory and History of Subcreation* was a huge inspiration for my first book, for which he very graciously wrote a cover blurb, and serves as the theoretical bedrock for the current work. To get to be a part of a series that excites me as a scholar and a reader is an academic dream come true, and I am indebted to Mark for his kindness and guidance, as well as for the incisive feedback he provided that made this book much stronger.

I am grateful to Dr. William Proctor for several email exchanges on the subject of reboots, retcons, and multiverses, which helped me think through a variety of the themes that recur in this book. Our fun and engaging conversations always energize me towards future projects, and I hope that one day we'll actually get to meet in person.

Perhaps my biggest thanks for the direction of this book must go to the anonymous reviewers of my proposal, whose inciteful critique helped me see that at the heart of an impossible attempt to shoehorn the entire history of DC Comics into 35,000 words was actually a much more sustainable, narrowly focused look at the DC Multiverse. At Routledge, Erica Wetter, Mia Moran, and especially Emma Sherriff have been of enormous help shepherding this book from conception to completion.

Finally, I must give my love and thanks to the many friends and family whose support enable me to be able to feel confident enough to ever put words down on the page, especially the Random Geeky group for lots of deep conversations about very shallow things, my co-workers at Software Advice and IBM for helping me to grow as a writer, and my colleagues hard at work in the trenches of academia who force me to examine the deeper purpose of everything I write.

Most importantly, I can never give enough appreciation to my parents, who have supported and encouraged me as a writer and scholar from the very beginning; to Aunt Marylin, my number-one cheerleader; and to Kaley, who reminds me every day that there's no place in the multiverse I'd rather be than by her side (though ideally I'd be by her side at Disney World).

Introduction

Towards the end of David Lindsay-Abaire's 2007 Pulitzer Prize-winning play *Rabbit Hole*, a middle-aged mother named Becca sits in her living room with a teenage boy. The boy, Jason, holds a tragic connection to Becca; several months earlier, he struck and killed Becca's young son in a car accident. Prior to this encounter, Jason had mailed Becca and her husband a short story he wrote about parallel universes. This leads the pair to the following exchange:

Becca: Is that something you believe in?
Jason: Parallel universes?
Becca: Yeah.
Jason: Sure. I mean, if space is infinite, which is what most scientists think, then yeah, there *have* to be parallel universes.
Becca: There *have* to be?
Jason: Yeah, because infinite space means . . . it means it goes on and on forever, so there's a never-ending stream of possibilities.
Becca: Okay.
Jason: So even the most unlikely events have to take place *somewhere*, including other universes with versions of us leading different lives, or maybe the same lives with a couple things changed.
Becca: And you think that's plausible.
Jason: Not just plausible—probable. If you accept the most basic laws of science.

(143–144)

What at first seems like something of a conversational tangent then turns into a serious discussion of the overwhelming sadness afflicting both characters:

Becca: So somewhere out there, there's a version of me—what—making pancakes?
Jason: Sure.
Becca: Or at a water park.
Jason: Wherever, yeah. Both. If space is infinite. Then there are tons of you's out there, and tons of me's.
Becca: And so this is just the sad version of us.
Jason: I guess.
Becca: But there are versions where everything goes our way.
Jason: Right.
Becca: And those other versions *exist*. They're not hypothetical, they're actual, *real* people.
Jason: Yeah, assuming you believe in science.
Becca: Well that's a nice thought. That somewhere out there I'm having a good time.

(144–145)

The scene ends shortly thereafter.

In this conversation about parallel universes, Becca and Jason are discussing the concept of a multiverse—the idea that our universe is just one of many universes. Though this idea is most familiar to many of us through fiction, it is also one that has a basis in cutting-edge scientific theory and exploration. For many scientists, the concept of the multiverse is intriguing from the perspective of a desire to know more about the structure of reality. Physicist Brian Greene, for example, notes in the introduction to his book about parallel worlds that "many of the major developments in fundamental theoretical physics . . . have led us to consider one or another variety of parallel universe. . . . It's at once humbling and stirring to imagine just how expansive reality may be" (5). Writers such as Lindsay-Abaire, on the other hand, are attracted to the poetic and aesthetic possibilities of multiple realities, each with a different version of the life we know.

Popular science writer John Gribbin unites these two perspectives when he notes that:

> the universe really could be infinite, even though we see only a finite volume. . . . An infinite number of worlds allows for an infinite number of variations and, indeed, an infinite number of identical copies. In that sense, in an infinite Universe, anything is possible, including an infinite number of other Earths where there are people identical to you and me going about their lives exactly as we do; and an infinite number of other Earths where you are Prime Minister and I am King. And so on.
>
> (8)

Unfortunately for anybody who would like to meet their own doppelgänger and see what life had been like had they worked up the courage to ask that special person to the prom, Gribbin goes on to explain that:

> the chances of any of these similar Earths occupying "our" bubble are vanishingly small. The nearest "other you" is likely to live in a bubble so far away that . . . to express it in metres you would need a number with 10^{29} zeroes.
>
> (8)

Thus, although the multiverse may indeed be science fact, it is left to the realm of science fiction to actually *explore* that multiverse, at least for the foreseeable future. Fortunately, creators of science fiction (and, as we saw in *Rabbit Hole*, also writers of a more literary bent) have been charting their visions of the multiverse for decades now. Whatever the distant future may hold for scientific expeditions into the "real" multiverse, for now, if we desire to explore the implications of the multiverse for the human mind, we must turn to the humanities, and particularly to the realm of speculative fiction.

The World of the DC Comics Multiverse

If there's one particular vision of a multiverse that's been charted and explored more than any other, it is likely the multiverse of super-hero adventures depicted in the pages of comic books published by DC Comics. Indeed, the DC Comics multiverse is one of the longest-lasting and most expansive story worlds in modern times.

From the publication of the first issue of *Detective Comics* in 1937 through to the present day, the comic books of DC and its corporate predecessors have slowly built up this multiverse, bit by bit and month after month. Certainly, the "world-building" aspects of the publisher's output were somewhat haphazard at first, but by the end of the 1960s and beginning of the 1970s, DC (in part copying the intentional world-building continuity of rival Marvel Comics) was working deliberately to create a cohesive story world spanning a multiverse full of different Earths.

In the world of DC Comics, the characters themselves are often aware of their existence within a multiverse. Different versions of those characters from several different universes frequently meet, cross over, and interact with one another. Although most of DC Comics' output at any time tends to focus on the heroes of one primary universe, many of the landmark moments in the history of DC Comics involve stories that revolve around the multiverse. What began as a bit of a slapdash connection between alternate versions of popular characters from different eras was refined, redefined, and retconned[1] continually over time such that ultimately readers could chart and follow a unified cosmology of fictional parallel worlds composing the entirety of creation (including our own "real" world, or at least a fictionalized version thereof).

DC Comics, though, was not the first fictional realm to feature the concept of a multiverse. The idea of "parallel universes" in science fiction goes back to at least the nineteenth century, and arguably all the way back to a variety of world mythologies. Writers such as John Cowper Powys and Michael Moorcock were developing their own unique multiverses of parallel universes roughly contemporaneously to DC. However, the writers, artists, and editors at DC were the first creators to *refine* that concept into a unique storytelling engine that allowed them to fill out not just an imaginary world, but entire imaginary *worlds*, full of characters, histories, geographies, religions, ethnographies, and so forth.

One of the most unique aspects of the DC Comics imaginary world, then, is its implementation and exploration of the multiverse concept on a huge scale, something that has since been copied in various other media, from television shows (*Sliders, Star Trek*, etc.), to novels (the works of Roger Zelazny and Philip José Farmer), to other comic book universes (particularly Marvel Comics). To study the history and implications of the DC Comics multiverse, then, is to explore the ways in which stories of parallel universes can come to play a crucial role in large-scale imaginary worlds.

Imaginary Multiverses

In *Building Imaginary Worlds: The Theory and History of Subcreation* (2012), media scholar Mark J.P. Wolf posits a theory of what he calls "imaginary worlds," defined as:

> All the surroundings and places experienced by a fictional charac-
> ter (or which could be experienced by one) that together constitute
> a unified sense of place which is ontologically different from the
> actual, material, and so-called "real" world. As "world" in this
> sense refers to an experiential realm, an imaginary world could be
> as large as a universe, or as small as an isolated town in which a
> character resides.[2]

(377)

Wolf makes the case that imaginary worlds are an interdisciplinary object of study that should be examined not just from one perspective, but rather through a variety of lenses, ranging from literary studies and history through to film studies and philosophy. He advocates for an interdisciplinary subfield of media studies geared towards studying "subcreation," author J.R.R. Tolkien's term for the creation of imagi-nary worlds. This is a worthwhile—and indeed necessary—pursuit because through examining the imaginary worlds in which we choose to spend our time, we learn more about what we want the "real" world (or, as Tolkien calls it, the Primary World) to look like. As Wolf writes:

> Subcreation is not just a desire, but a need and a right; it renews our vision and gives us new perspective and insight into the ontological questions that might otherwise escape our notice within the default assumptions we make about reality. Subcreated worlds also direct our attention beyond themselves, moving us beyond the quotidian and the material, increasing our awareness of how we conceptualize, understand, and imagine the Primary World.
>
> (287)

In the tradition of all fantastical stories going back for millennia, today's imaginary worlds provide a valuable tool to understanding our own cultural concerns and moral quandaries. The DC Comics multiverse is no different.

Though it consists of an (at times) infinite number of different parallel worlds—Wolf defines a multiverse as "the overall structure resulting from the connection of two or more universes that, though connected, still remain distinct and different" (218)—taken as a whole the DC Comics multiverse can be considered as one "imaginary world," in Wolf's sense. It is, however, an imaginary world that focuses on multiplicity, exploring its characters and its narratives through the lens of different iterations of how those narratives, and thus those characters, might have unfolded. While one version of Superman may be young, naive, and single, able to defeat any foe save for the heartsickness he feels knowing he can never reveal his secrets to Lois Lane, another version can be older, married to Lois, and have a child with her, providing different insights into the iconic character. Thus, the multiverse found in the imaginary world of DC Comics is an expansive structure allowing for the creation of further "realms of possibility, a mix of familiar and unfamiliar, permutations of wish, dread, and dream" (Wolf 17).

Grant Morrison, one of several creators who has attempted to completely map the DC Multiverse, notes another important aspect of the multiverse—it provides the opportunity for a great deal of fun. He explains:

> I think it's just a primal thing, seeing the variants of characters—seeing the versions of things. . . . We've often thought of alternative versions of our own lives, so I think people like to read about these characters having alternative lives and taking different paths and making different choices.
>
> (quoted in Martin)

This exploration of alternative choices is an essential quality of the DC Multiverse, one that accounts for its continual return even as various editorial administrations at DC Comics have attempted to clean up the narrative confusions that tend to surround these infinite worlds.

In their introduction to a collection of essays about world-building, Pat Harrigan and Noah Wardrip-Fruin describe the DC multiverse as something that allows for:

> differently branded versions of DC characters to appear in nonoverlapping (and noncontradictory) story lines, considered to be happening in parallel universes. . . . There is no contradiction between these various versions of characters, because they are not considered, among DC readers or creators, to be "in the same universe."
>
> (6)

Harrigan and Wardrip-Fruin go on to note that:

> This may seem like a lot of heavy labor to justify the ontological status of imaginary stories, but the fact is that this is the inescapable result of a vast narrative spread over time that by necessity involves many of the same elements (characters particularly) in perpetual novel deployment. Sooner or later, you have to invent the ground rules for the stories you want to tell.
>
> (6)

The DC Multiverse, then, provides the "ground rules" for the multitude of stories set in DC Comics' imaginary world.

Though the DC Multiverse primarily exists as a setting for narratives, it also exists as a kind of map of the entire imaginary world of DC Comics. By allowing for multiplicity, the multiverse gives creators the ability to continually flesh out the details of this infinitely expansive imaginary world, creating a massive structure within which endless narrative permutations can take place, from the prosaic to the bombastic, many of which pay homage to the company's long legacy of heroic creations. Given the nature of DC Comics' existence as a publisher of superhero stories, that is the primary narrative genre that dominates, but over the course of its history DC has also produced war stories, westerns, romance comics, and so forth, many of which have later been subsumed into the omnivorous expansion of the multiverse, which seems able to accommodate nearly every story DC has ever published by simply placing it in one universe or another.

It is indeed this aspect of the multiverse that makes it so important to the DC Comics imaginary world. It aids the writers, artists, editors, and other creators in maintaining, according to Wolf, the "three main properties needed to produce a secondary world, hold it together, and make it distinct from the Primary World" (33): invention, completeness, and consistency. In regard to invention—"the degree to which default assumptions based on the Primary World have been changed, regarding such things as geography, history, language, physics, biology, zoology, culture, custom, and so on" (34)—the multiverse provides the opportunities for creators to chart and explore worlds that differ from our own in ways that the main DC universe, designed to simulate the world outside our windows (save for the existence of superheroes, magic, aliens, and the like), does not. The multiverse also aids in this imaginary world's completeness—"the degree to which the world contains explanations and details covering all the various aspects of its characters' experiences, as well as background details which together suggest a feasible, practical world" (38)—by creating a larger cosmology of the fantastic that posits the extraordinary and fantastic as "normal," with worlds such as our "real" world the outlier rather than the norm. Finally, and perhaps most of all, the multiverse provides the imaginary world of DC Comics with a larger sense of consistency—"the degree to which world details are plausible, feasible, and without contradiction" (43)—by providing a useful scapegoat for contradictory stories. The multiverse frequently provides an easy out for creators to fix up continuity problems, relegating those contradictory stories to different universes.

Ironically, it is that same urge to clear up continuity via the multiverse that often leads to even further contradictions, requiring bigger, more complex stories to tie up loose ends and "fix" the multiverse. The history of the DC Multiverse is one of confusion, clutter, and giant, eschatological "events" that every so often recreate and rewrite the multiverse entirely. This serves as a strategy of rejuvenation, for the worlds of the multiverse and the characters within them as well as for the creators and readers in the Primary World. The multiverse is not just a static map or guidebook in which creators can place characters and stories (though there *are* maps and guidebooks); it is, in many ways, a living, breathing entity that changes every time a new piece of story or world-building is added to it. According to Grant Morrison, the world of DC Comics is not just a fiction, but rather:

> exists within our own universe. . . . The ground of being of the DC Universe is the white page before anything's drawn on it. . . . The universe exists on the second dimension and we can read their adventures with Superman going back to 1938, and you can put them all together and look at them from above.
>
> (quoted in Martin)

Though Morrison takes this concept to the extreme, it is vital to DC Comics' imaginary world that it is an "open world," described by Wolf as "a world in which canonical material is still being added; such a world is still growing and developing, as it accrues more information, detail, and narrative" (270). DC Comics (along with most comic book universes) is somewhat unique among imaginary worlds in that there isn't one single creator who's the fountainhead from which the universe springs, as with, for example, George Lucas and *Star Wars* or J.R.R. Tolkien and *The Lord of the Rings*. Rather, though individual characters have specific creators, the larger world and the concepts and characters therein have evolved slowly over the better part of a century as details are added, bedrock concepts concretized, and initially independent narratives tied together into a cohesive, if at times incomprehensible, multiverse.

If current cutting-edge astrophysics is to be believed, though, the DC multiverse isn't alone in its many confusions; we may indeed be living within a complex, evolving multiverse of our own.

The Science and Philosophy of the Multiverse

Although we may be most familiar with the concept of a multiverse through the realm of science fiction, there is increasingly a body of literature based in scientific fact that posits that we live inside of an actual multiverse ourselves. As physicist Michio Kaku notes:

> The very idea of parallel universes was once viewed with suspicion by scientists as being the province of mystics, charlatans, and cranks. Any scientist daring to work on parallel universes was subject to ridicule and was jeopardizing his or her career, since even today there is no experimental evidence proving their existence. But recently, the tide has turned dramatically, with the finest minds on the planet working furiously on the subject. The reason for this sudden change is the arrival of a new theory, string theory, and its latest version, M-theory, which promise . . . to unravel the nature of the multiverse.

(16)

However, it remains very unclear precisely what that multiverse will actually look like.

In his history of research into the multiverse, fittingly titled *In Search of the Multiverse* (2009), John Gribbin explains that the first use of the word "multiverse" can be found in the writings of psychologist William James. However, as Gribbin explains, James:

was interested in mysticism and religious experiences, not the nature of the physical Universe. Similarly, although the word appears in the writings of G.K. Chesterton, John Cowper Powys and Michael Moorcock, none of this has any relevance to its use in a scientific context.

(9)

The first scientific conception of a multiverse would be Hugh Everett III's "many worlds interpretation," developed in the 1950s. Everett theorized, according to Gribbin, that there is a:

"splitting" of an observer whenever a quantum measurement ... is made.... Both outcomes are equally likely, so both are equally real.... [T]he entire Universe, including the observer, splits.... Everett's great achievement was to express this in accurate mathematical language.

(26)

However, the actual word "multiverse" wouldn't emerge in that context until the 1960s (around the same time that DC's multiverse was born), and it would not come to hold its current scientific meaning until David Deutsch's 1997 book *The Fabric of Reality*. Gribbin explains that the way Deutsch defines the word multiverse—"to denote physical reality as a whole"—is "now the way it is used by all scientists interested in the idea of other worlds. The Multiverse is everything that there is; a universe is a portion of the Multiverse accessible to a particular set of observers" (10–11).

The way that scientists envision this multiverse of "everything that there is," however, can vary greatly between different theories. In his book *The Hidden Reality: Parallel Universes and the Deep Laws of the Cosmos* (2011), Brian Greene traces nine distinct "variations on the multiverse theme," each of which:

envisions our universe as part of an unexpectedly larger whole, but the complexion of that whole and the nature of the member universes differ sharply among them. In some, the parallel universes are separated from us by enormous stretches of space or time; in others, they're hovering millimeters away; in others still, the very notion of their location proves parochial, devoid of meaning. A similar range of possibility is manifest in the laws governing the parallel universes. In some, the laws are the same as in ours; in others, they appear different but have a shared heritage; in others still, the laws are of a form and structure unlike anything we've ever encountered.

(5)

With such a range of expansive possibilities to the "real" multiverse, it's no wonder that the creators of DC Comics' multiverse utilize the concept of parallel worlds for expansive story ideas encompassing multiple variations of familiar characters under unfamiliar conditions.

However, not all multiversal theories are created equal. Though physicist Steven Manly claims that "the multiverse is here to stay," he clarifies that "the question is not 'Do we live in a multiverse?' Rather the questions are 'Do we live in multiple types of universes?' and, if so, 'Which ones?'" (232–234). Some of the current theories of the multiverse will likely one day be proven scientifically invalid. What will remain important and vital, though, are the ways in which humanity reacts to and plays with the idea of the multiverse, however it is configured.

In her in-depth examination of the philosophical and theological ramifications of the multiverse upon human thought, *Worlds Without End: The Many Lives of the Multiverse* (2014), religious studies scholar Mary-Jane Rubenstein notes that this century's scientific interest in the multiverse "has in turn led to a renewed proliferation of pop-cultural explorations of hidden dimensions, parallel universes, and copycat cosmoi" (1). Seen through this lens, it is perhaps no coincidence that the same year in which *Worlds Without End* was released, 2014, also saw the publication of *The Multiversity*, one of DC Comics' most explicit deep dives into the core of its own multiverse concept. Rubenstein argues that:

In promising a view from nowhere that gets rid of God *and* accounts for every possible everything, the multiverse seems to promise the ultimate scientific vision of reality. . . . At this point, it once again becomes very hard to argue that any of these visions of reality genuinely frees modern science from philosophy and religion—not least because they all seek the ultimate, objective *truth* of creation.

(233)

This, too, is reflected in DC Comics. The tangled history of the DC Multiverse is intimately tied with the search (by characters and creators alike) for that multiverse's origins, a question that cuts to the heart of multiversal cosmology. The multiverse, then, simultaneously embraces the chaos of multiplicity and the order of a search for meaning. Rubenstein notes that what she finds most promising is not actually the answers to any questions about the multiverse:

> but the processes that produce and undo them: those endless cosmogonic efforts to derive *all this* from *that*, efforts whose very multiplicity signal a persistence of chaos amid anything that looks like order. And such persistence, I think, is the real promise of the multiverse. Tuned in to the background noise of many-world cosmologies—of their failure to disentangle physics from metaphysics from religion from science—entangles the one and the many; of an "order" constituted, dismantled, and renewed by an ever-roiling chaos; of a "truth" that remains provisional, multiple, and perspectival; and, perhaps, of a theology that asks more interesting and more pressing questions than whether the universe has been "designed" by an anthropomorphic, extracosmic deity.

(236)

Such questions regarding the DC Multiverse are continually asked, answered, invalidated, re-asked, reanswered, and so forth in a procession of stories that evolve the multiverse to fit the tastes of contemporary readers. However, this is not the only (nor even the first) multiverse to pose such questions about order, chaos, and the nature of existence itself.

Moorcock's Multiverses

Though several prominent science-fiction and fantasy writers—such as Robert Heinlein, Terry Pratchett, and John Cowper Powys—have created a multiverse that links together their various works, perhaps no other writer is as prominently associated with this concept as Michael Moorcock. Over more than half a century, Moorcock's wide variety of interconnected novels, short stories, and comic books have explored the ways in which a multiverse can take on deeper metaphorical meanings beyond just serving as a narrative structure, something that the DC Comics Multiverse has also achieved over roughly the same period.

Moorcock's first mention of a multiverse came in his 1965 novel *The Sundered Worlds*, a relatively straightforward, pulpy science-fiction story that introduces the idea of spaceships with the ability to travel between dimensions. During one such transition between universes, Moorcock describes the multiverse as follows:

> Finite, yet containing the stuff of infinity, the multiverse wheeled in its gigantic movement through space. To those who could observe it from beyond its boundaries . . . it appeared as a solid construction, dense and huge. Yet within it there were many things, many intelligences who did not realise that they dwelt in the multiverse, since each layer was separated from another by dimensions. Dimensions that were like leaves between the layers. Here and there the mighty structure was flawed—by fragments which moved *through* the dimensions, through the leaves, passing many universes; by a vacuum existing where one small part had vanished. But, on the whole, the universes remained unknown to one another. They did not realise they were part of a composite structure of fantastic complexity. They did not realise their purpose or the purpose for which the multiverse had been created. Only the chosen knew—and of them only a few understood.
>
> (86)

In this passage, Moorcock sets out the basic terms of the multiverse as he would come to chart it over the ensuing decades, always with an eye towards using it to explore deeper truths about the human condition and the purpose of being alive.

As he continued to flesh out his multiverse, Moorcock would intimately tie it to other recurring motifs in his work, such as an "Eternal Champion" reincarnated through a thousand lifetimes to fight for the "Cosmic Balance" between "Law" and "Chaos" as a part of the "Game of Time." As Moorcock describes it:

> I use the idea of Law and Chaos precisely because I am suspicious of simplistic notions of good and evil. In my multiverse, Law and Chaos are both legitimate ways of interpreting and defining experience. Ideally, the Cosmic Balance keeps both sides in equilibrium. By playing 'the Game of Time' . . . the various participants maintain that equilibrium.
>
> (1994, vii)

Within this larger philosophical cosmology, the multiverse:

> is a multitude of alternative universes intersecting sometimes with our own and to which, of course, our own belongs—an infinite number of slightly different versions of oneself. In its more sophisticated use this enables me to deal in non-linear terms with varieties of perception, to make, in the few didactic books I've written, simplified models of ideal worlds to show, I hope, by what particular injustices and hypocrisies those worlds might be maintained. By using these devices to connect one book with another, I hope to look at a number of different aspects of the same theme while firmly linking the most outrageous fables with experiences of the world we all share. Thanks to these ideas, I have characters who can move easily between this world and all the others without any sense of discrepancy or incoherence.
>
> (1994, ix)

Given the number of hands that have been involved in its creation, the DC Multiverse adheres to no such similar set of philosophical standards as Moorcock's does, but his explanation here shows the important ways in which such a construct can be used in an imaginary world.

As is the case with the DC Multiverse, in the Moorcock multiverse it is the sense of multiplicity, variation, and repetition that invokes pleasure in readers and creator alike. As literary scholar Mark Scroggins notes:

> What Moorcock in essence has done, in arguing that his works together present pictures of a single multiverse, is to provide a scientific (or science-fictional) rationalization for the thematic continuities of his created worlds. They are similar because they are related, a "near infinity of space-time continua each fractionally different"—and to a greater or lesser degree alike. . . . The central figure of the Eternal Champion remains in place, in different avatars in different sequences, but Moorcock will repeatedly evoke a frisson of pleasant recognition in his readers by recycling antagonists and supporting characters, by playing variations upon previously presented narrative situations, and even by putting more than one Champion avatar on stage at the same time.
>
> (22–23)

As I will show throughout this book, various creators working for DC Comics have attempted to achieve similar results in their own explorations of the publisher's multiverse.

What's more, while Moorcock typically can only rely on rich, descriptive prose to describe the cosmic nature of his multiverse, DC's multiverse has the added power of a visual component, something that plays as crucial a role in the history of the multiverse as the narrative storylines themselves. Perhaps it is no surprise, then, that the work in which Moorcock most directly mines the interwoven nature of his multiverse of worlds and characters comes in the form of a 12-issue comic book series, *Michael Moorcock's Multiverse*, published by none other than DC Comics.

Outline

This book is roughly divided into two halves. The first two chapters will take a chronological approach to exploring how the DC Comics Multiverse evolved over time in various comic books produced by the publisher, focusing on key story points over the company's almost 90-year history. The next two chapters, as well as the conclusion, will move away from this historical approach and instead examine several key case studies and look at the lasting impact of the DC Multiverse on other comic book publishers and creators of imaginary worlds, as well as studying transmedia adaptations of DC's multiverse into other media.

Chapter 1 will explore the slow creation of the DC Comics Multiverse over the course of the publisher's first 40 years of stories. This was the "first phase" of the DC Multiverse, which featured ever-more parallel worlds added to an increasingly complex cosmology. It was during this time that DC first exploited the possibilities inherent in a multiverse, with multiple versions of familiar characters featured in different storylines and ongoing series, and other characters moving between universes with great regularity. This chapter will take a deep dive into what media scholar Henry Jenkins has termed comics' discovery "that readers take great pleasure in encountering and comparing multiple versions of the same characters" (307).

The second chapter will pick up from the first in exploring the "second phase" of DC's multiverse, which began in 1985 with the crossover series *Crisis on Infinite Earths*. *Crisis* attempted to make DC's stories less confusing and more accessible to readers by consolidating the multiverse into a single cohesive universe. However, many creators still working for DC, then and in the years to follow, bucked against this editorial decision, and worked to bring back elements of the multiverse and DC's many parallel universes, ultimately culminating (about 20 years later) with the return of the multiverse in *Infinite Crisis*, the sequel to *Crisis on Infinite Earths*. Since then, creators have once again played with the storytelling possibilities of the multiverse, with some even making it a hallmark of their work for the publisher.

In the third chapter, I take a closer look at the work of four writers whose additions to DC Comics helped to define the cosmology and parameters of its multiverse—Gardner Fox, Marv Wolfman, Geoff Johns, and Grant Morrison. By taking case studies from each of their work, I will be able to examine the specific ways in which they exploited, added to, and in some cases redefined how the DC

Multiverse functions as a crucial aspect of the publisher's larger imaginary world.

Chapter 4 looks at the impact of DC's multiverse on other comic book publishers (especially their main competitor Marvel Comics) and on the wider world of genre fiction in general. This will include the ways in which DC's multiverse has been translated into multimedia iterations of DC's characters and world, such as animation, television series, and even novels. By examining how the concept of the multiverse spread to other media and forms, I make the case for the impact that DC Comics has had on the development of this tool of storytelling and world-building.

The conclusion takes this last point even further and makes several suggestions of what world-builders/subcreators can learn from the DC Multiverse in order to create richer, deeper, more densely populated imaginary worlds of their own. It is my hope, then, that learning more about the DC Multiverse will provide inspiration to artists, writers, scholars, and other subcreators who want to invent and develop their own imaginary worlds in order to help "re-enchant" the Primary World in which we live, by creating alternate realities through which we might see a path to a future more rife with possibility than our present.

Notes

1 Short for "retroactive continuity," which I have defined elsewhere as "a narrative process wherein the creator(s) and/or producer(s) of a fictional narrative/world—often, but not always, the same person or people—deliberately alter the history of that narrative/world such that, going forward, future stories reflect this *new* history, completely ignoring the old as if it had never happened" (Friedenthal 7).
2 Historian Michael Saler evocatively calls these imaginary worlds "public spheres of the imagination." He notes, "These fantastic, cohesive, and virtual worlds had personal, social, and political consequences. They provided new social networks, countering the disenchanting effects of isolation and anomie that modernity could engender." Furthermore, and perhaps most applicable to the DC Multiverse, "The alternate realities posited by these virtual worlds had their own ambiguities, and the conflicting interpretations generated in public spheres of the imagination habituated readers to see narratives as complex, provisional, and pragmatic, rather than as transparent, essential, and unchanging" (17–19).

References

Friedenthal, Andrew. *Retcon Game: Retroactive Continuity and the Hyperlinking of America*. Jackson, MS: University Press of Mississippi, 2017.

Greene, Brian. *The Hidden Reality: Parallel Universes and the Deep Laws of the Cosmos*. New York: Vintage Books, 2011.

Gribbin, John. *In Search of the Multiverse: Parallel Worlds, Hidden Dimensions, and the Ultimate Quest for the Frontiers of Reality*. Hoboken, NJ: John Wiley & Sons, 2009.

Harrigan, Pat and Noah Wardrip-Fruin. "Introduction." In *Third Person: Authoring and Exploring Vast Narratives*, edited by Pat Harrigan and Noah Wardrip-Fruin. Cambridge, MA: MIT Press, 2009.

Jenkins, Henry. "Managing Multiplicity in Superhero Comics." In *Third Person: Authoring and Exploring Vast Narratives*, edited by Pat Harrigan and Noah Wardrip-Fruin. Cambridge, MA: MIT Press, 2009.

Kaku, Michio. *Parallel Worlds: A Journey Through Creation, Higher Dimensions, and the Future of the Cosmos*. New York: Anchor Books, 2005.

Lindsay-Abaire, David. *Rabbit Hole*. New York: Theatre Communications Group, 2006.

Manly, Steven. *Visions of the Multiverse*. Pompton Plains, NJ: New Page Books, 2011.

Martin, Garrett. "Grant Morrison Merges String Theory with Superheroes in DC's *Multiversity*." *Paste*. Last modified August 20, 2014. www.pastemagazine.com/articles/2014/08/across-the-universes-grant-morrison-merges-string.html.

Moorcock, Michael. "Introduction." In *The Eternal Champion*. Clarkston, GA: White Wolf, 1994.

Moorcock, Michael. *The Sundered Worlds*. New York: Paperback Library, 1966.

Rubenstein, Mary-Jane. *Worlds Without End: The Many Lives of the Multiverse*. New York: Columbia University Press, 2014.

Saler, Michael. *As If: Modern Enchantment and the Literary Prehistory of Virtual Reality*. Oxford: Oxford University Press, 2012.

Scroggins, Mark. *Michael Moorcock: Fiction, Fantasy and the World's Pain*. Jefferson, NC: McFarland & Company, 2015.

Wolf, Mark J.P. *Building Imaginary Worlds: The Theory and History of Subcreation*. New York: Routledge, 2012.

1 A Brief History of the Multiverse

Before there could be a DC Multiverse, the DC Universe had to come into being. In the early days of the comics industry, and the burgeoning popularity of the superhero genre, such an occurrence was itself a novelty.

With the publication of the first Superman story in 1938's *Action Comics* #1 by what was then known as National Allied Publications, the world was first exposed to the concept of the superhero[1]—a genre that would soon prove to be the most popular form of storytelling in the comic book medium. Writer Jerry Siegel and artist Joe Schuster had together created a phenomenon, and Superman proved to be just the first of many heroes published by National (which changed its name to DC Comics in 1940), its sister company All-American Comics (which would later get folded into the DC Comics publishing line), and numerous other publishers that had popped up in the first few years of the comic book industry. By the end of 1940, All-American had so many heroes that editor Sheldon Mayer and writer Gardner Fox hit upon what was, at the time, a unique idea—to bring all their biggest heroes together into one story, united under the banner of the "Justice Society of America."

Paul Levitz—comic book creator, former DC Comics president/publisher, and author of the company's officially sanctioned history, *75 Years of DC Comics* (2010)—explains just how revolutionary this concept was in its time:

In popular culture today, the idea of a crossover permeates television, film, and novels, and is one of the great engines of comics . . . but in 1941, the idea of mixing separate properties together was radical . . . and an enduring enough hit that *Justice Society of America* (*JSA*) ran to the end of the Golden Age.

$(56)^2$

By joining together the company's most popular characters into one team, Mayer and Fox created the concept of the fully interlinked comic book universe. Although individual authors—most notably L. Frank Baum and Edgar Rice Burroughs—had by this point brought together several of their own separate imaginary worlds, this was the first time that such a crossover of characters and worlds was happening in the genre of superhero comics. These early Justice Society stories were very light on continuity, but they did reflect changes in costume and concept from the characters' own books, giving birth to the idea that these stories all took place in the same world.

Thus was the DC Universe born. It would not be until 20 years later that this universe finally expanded into a multiverse, one that endured—in what I call the "first phase" of the DC Multiverse—until the mid-1980s.

The Flash of Two Worlds

The popularity of the superhero lasted throughout World War II, but it began to lose its luster in the postwar years. Because comic books had been sent in care packages to soldiers overseas, many of the young servicemen came home as ardent readers, but they longed for stories and genres that were more complex than the simple good-versus-evil fisticuffs that dominated the superhero comics. Genres such as war, crime, and horror became bestsellers, and most of the early superhero comics of the era, which has in retrospect been named the "Golden Age," were cancelled one by one.[3]

Then, in 1954, the comics industry was rocked by a Senate subcommittee hearing on whether or not comic books inspired juvenile delinquency. In order to get ahead of any potential government censorship (and, some critics argue, to curtail the success of publisher EC Comics, which thrived thanks to producing more adult material), the leading publishers banded together to form their own self-censoring organization, the Comics Code Authority (CCA). In the aftermath of the CCA's formation, comics became children's fare once more, with simplistic moral tales full of gentle comedy and limited action— perfect for the superhero genre to make a resurgence.[4]

Such, at least, was the thinking of DC Comics editor Julius Schwartz, when in 1956 he hired writer Bob Kanigher and artist Carmine Infantino to create a new version of one of DC's classic heroes, the super-speedster known as the Flash. Whereas the Flash of the Golden Age had been a college student named Jay Garrick, this new creation was more in step with the science-obsessed postwar years. Barry Allen was a police scientist who gained super-speed when lighting struck his laboratory and doused him in chemicals. As Levitz again points out, this revival (which began what some fans and historians now call the "Silver Age" of comics) was revolutionary in its time:

> From a 21st-century perspective, with the word "reboot" now in common language, it's hard to consider how radical the changes in Schwartz's revival were, as he chose to keep the name, emblem, and essential powers of the original and tossed the rest of the elements away.
>
> (250)

In a unique twist, though, Allen was actually *inspired* by Jay Garrick's adventures, which he read about in a comic book. Though this meta-textual twist was likely more of an in-joke, a knowing nod for fans old enough to remember the Golden Age Flash, it would ultimately prove to be the first glimmering of the DC Multiverse.

That glimmering was finally brought to full light in 1961, with issue 123 of *The Flash*, titled "Flash of Two Worlds!"[5] In this story, while entertaining a group of orphans in the Central City Community Center, Barry Allen ends up moving so quickly that he finds himself in an alternate dimension. When he discovers that he is not in Central City, but rather a place called Keystone City, he remembers that this was the name of the city where Jay Garrick lived in the comic books Barry read as a child. He looks up Jay in the phone book and surprises the older Flash at home, explaining that, "The way I see it, I vibrated so fast—I tore a gap in the vibratory shields separating our worlds! As you know—two objects can occupy the same space and time—if they vibrate at different speeds!" (13).

It is this scientifically dubious concept—that objects can occupy the same space and time by vibrating at different speeds—that becomes the cornerstone of the DC Multiverse. As Barry goes on to explain:

> My theory is, both Earths were created at the same time in two quite similar universes! They vibrate differently—which keeps them apart! Life, customs—even languages—evolved on your Earth almost exactly as they did on my Earth! Destiny must have decreed there'd be a Flash—on each Earth! . . . I became the super-fast Flash on my Earth much as you became the Flash on yours! Indeed, reading of your Flash adventures inspired me to assume the secret identity of the Flash! . . . You were once well-known in my world—as a fictional character appearing in a magazine called *Flash Comics*! When I was a youngster—you were my favorite hero! A writer named Gardner Fox wrote about your adventures—which he claimed came to him in dreams! Obviously when Fox was asleep, his mind was "tuned in" on your vibratory Earth! That explains how he "dreamed up" the Flash! The magazine was discontinued in 1949!
>
> (14–15)

Jay replies to this revelation by noting that 1949 was the year he retired from active duty as the Flash, providing the first indication of another "scientific" hallmark of DC's multiverse—that time moves differently on different worlds, so that duplicates of the same hero (and even duplicates of the same person, as would later become clear) age at different rates, allowing for older and younger versions to coexist across the multiple Earths.

In this initial description, we already see two themes that would become crucial to the DC Multiverse: multiplicity and legacy. By presenting two versions of the same hero (even though they had different secret identities), the Flashes of two worlds showcased how the DC Multiverse could accommodate more than just one type of hero. While Barry represented the young, single, adventure-driven kind of hero that had become the norm in DC Comics by this time, Jay was an elder statesman, a retiree in a stable marriage who was still able to fight the forces of evil when called upon to do so (as he would be later in the story). While these multiple Flashes thus represented two types of heroes, which might appeal to two types of readers, they also highlighted the legacy of heroic deeds at DC Comics. In meeting Barry Allen, Jay Garrick was able to create a heroic legacy by passing on the mantle of the Flash to a younger generation, a theme that would recur in DC Comics going forward.

Not only did this create a thematic continuity between the two distinct versions of the Flash, but it also, according to scholar Angela Ndalianis:

> opened the way to, partially, rationalizing the contradictions and conflicts that had been created over many decades of tellings and retellings of superhero stories across the DC Universe. . . . Following this issue of *Flash*, the concept of the multiverse opened the way to the possibility of multiple story continuities, which could then be rationalized as belonging to alternate worlds. . . . Instead of refusing to acknowledge the existence of the other story, each new story thread acknowledges those that lie beneath it even if it is to reject it. Like the shifting continuities and the intertextual web of narrative threads that connect, or fail to connect, them, as more stories entered the arena the continuities (and the multiverse system that contained them) became far more elaborate.

(278–279)

"Flash of Two Worlds!" then, was the first building block in a multiverse that allowed various, originally unrelated story continuities to become subsumed into the imaginary world of DC Comics and henceforth serve as part of its history and legacy.

The theme of legacy was carried further in the very next encounter between the two Flashes, issue #129's "Double Danger on Earth!" In this story, we learn that Jay has permanently come out of retirement following his encounter with Barry, and over the course of about two pages he recalls the last time he wore his costumer prior to that momentous event—the final case of the Justice Society of America. *The Flash* #137—"Vengeance of the Immortal Villain!"—would go even further towards bringing back the JSA by featuring the team's other members as captives of one of their old villains, Vandal Savage. After the two Flashes rescue the JSA, Wonder Woman ponders aloud, "You know boys—I've been thinking—it might be a good idea for us to meet every so often—come out of retirement, as it were—to prevent anything like this from happening again!" (81–82).

With that, the Justice Society of America, the original superhero team (by this point there was a similar team-up of DC's current roster of heroes—including that Earth's Wonder Woman—in the form of the Justice *League* of America), returned to an active role in the DC Multiverse, tying the ongoing story world to its early roots. In many ways, though, "Vengeance of the Immortal Villain!" was just a prologue to a much bigger story, one that would fully take up the themes of multiplicity and legacy.

Crisis on Multiple Earths

The cover to 1963's *Justice League of America* #21—drawn by regular series penciller Mike Sekowsky—is notable for several reasons. First, it kicks off what would become a long tradition in DC Comics crossover stories of featuring as many characters as possible on one cover. In this image, Sekowsky shows the members of the Justice League of America (JLA), composed of the most popular heroes among DC's current roster—Superman, Batman, the Atom, Martian Manhunter, Wonder Woman, Green Lantern, Aquaman, and Green Arrow—conducting a seance around their meeting table. A billow of smoke arises from the crystal ball in the center of the table, out of which arise the figures of the Justice Society—Hawkman, Dr. Fate, Black Canary,

Hourman, and the Earth-Two Green Lantern and Atom. The cover copy is just as important to the history of the DC Multiverse in that it introduces a word that will come to be permanently associated with DC's biggest crossover series: "Crisis." Here, the word appears inside of a small box that gives the title of the issue as "Crisis on Earth-One!" alongside a separate box that proclaims, "Back after 12 years! The legendary super-stars of the Justice Society of America!" (5). Here, we see multiplicity and legacy combined into one key image and a pronouncement of the triumphant return of a classic superhero team.

The story within, once again written by Gardner Fox (as we will see in Chapter 3, Fox was one of the crucial figures in creating/exploring the DC Multiverse), opens with both the JLA and JSA on their respective Earths discussing challenges they've received from a team-up of some of their respective enemies. Though the JLA meeting is presented as nothing unusual for the team, the JSA's meeting is given much more weight by the description, both in captions and dialogue, that this is the team's first gathering since emerging from retirement. As one caption excitedly notes, "Yes, after more than a decade of inactivity—the old Justice Society of America is meeting once again! True, there are a few gray hairs showing—and their faces are lined with the passage of time—but their powers are only slightly dimmed" (8).

The two teams go on to encounter their foes only to see them disappear just prior to being captured. This turns out to be part of a scheme hatched by the combined teams of villains, who happened to encounter one another when Jay Garrick's old foe the Fiddler struck a particular vibration on his superpowered violin that transported him to Barry Allen's Earth. It is, in fact, the Fiddler who first refers to Barry's Earth as Earth-One (a curious choice for somebody from the dimension he himself relegates to "Earth-Two"), as do the rest of the characters throughout the story. This numerical ranking is clearly based on the fact that the creators and editors working at DC wanted to make no mistake about which was the Earth featured in their stories: Earth-One is the home of the primary DC Universe, while Earth-Two is the home of the older heroes who were written out of current continuity but whose appearances might appeal to longtime fans.

It isn't until the end of the issue that the two teams actually encounter one another, when the JLA contact the JSA through a magical seance and swap Earths in order to combat their foes, who have also exchanged home dimensions in order to go on crime sprees. The story continues into the next issue (entitled, fittingly, "Crisis on Earth-Two!"), something that itself was unusual in an era where most superhero tales concluded in one issue or less. *Justice League of America* #22 shows the heroes of the two Earths battling their enemies, only to each meet defeat and "find themselves locked inside cages— far out in the depths of space" (51). Until this point, both teams have fought separately, but in the final six pages of this second part of the story the JLA and JSA finally team up to escape their confinement, and in a dialogue-free double-page spread they work together to take down their foes. In a brief one-panel coda, the JSA's Hawkman tells the JLA, "We're going to keep in touch! There's no telling when we may be called upon to join forces again!" (56). This almost offhanded piece of dialogue, whether or not Fox intended it to do so, would soon become DC Comics gospel.

The First Phase of the DC Multiverse

The "Crisis on Earth-One!"/"Crisis on Earth-Two!" story proved to be so popular with fans, and such a sales success, that it would become an annual tradition. Each summer, the creators of the *Justice League of America* would craft a cross-Earth team-up with the Justice Society. As comics writer Mark Waid notes in his introduction to the first collection of these annual get-togethers, the stories were not just a sales gimmick, but also an opportunity to introduce or reintroduce characters into the larger tapestry of the multiverse:

> With each exciting exploit—or "crisis," as was invariably reflected in the story's title—the JSA enjoyed more and more of the limelight. . . . Summer "crises" were a guaranteed sales event that never grew stale; because the membership of the JSA was much larger and more fluid than the JLA's, every year afforded Schwartz

and Fox their chance to reintroduce a fresh handful of Golden Age characters—and by 1973, once all of Earth-Two's defenders had been pressed into service, Schwartz and his writers began stretching the dimensional boundaries to regularly incorporate the "forgotten" heroes of other "Earths." . . . As it happened, the dimensional void apparently contained an *infinite* number of worlds . . .

(4)

The regular tradition, then, became a cornerstone of one of DC's most important titles, *Justice League of America*, a series that served as the main showcase for the ways in which the publisher's individual characters and storylines converged into a larger imaginary world. By making the JLA/JSA team-up a crucial aspect of that series, DC was in effect putting the concept of the multiverse at the center of that story world, and some of the publisher's most famous stories (as well as the ones that did the most to contribute to DC's overall world-building) were a part of this tradition.

The second meeting of the two teams was notable for expanding the multiverse beyond just Earth-One and Earth-Two. What might have simply been a conceit by which DC could reintroduce older versions of characters without crowding out their current heroic stars, an idea potentially limited to just the two different worlds, took a leap forward with the appearance of Earth-Three, a dimension that was full of new creations who added to the multiplicity inherent in the DC Multiverse. The first character of this new Earth to appear in the story (entitled "Crisis on Earth-Three!") is, fittingly, that universe's version of the Flash, who in this case has taken the name "Johnny Quick." As we quickly learn, though, he is no heroic doppelgänger, but rather a villainous version of Jay Garrick and Barry Allen. An omniscient caption over a series of panels depicting skewed historical events relates the history of Earth-Three:

On Earth-1 and Earth-2, things are quite similar. Some superheroes have the same names, although they may not look alike. . . . But Earth-3! Woww! History repeats itself—in a reverse way! For instance, Columbus did not discover America! Columbus was an American—who discovered Europe! Not only that—but colonial England won her freedom from the United States in the Revolutionary War of 1776 . . . and it was actor Abe Lincoln who shot President John Wilkes Booth! . . . Small wonder, then, that there are no super-heroes on Earth-3! For Earth-3 is a world where every super-being is a criminal—who have banded themselves together to form the Crime Syndicate of America!

(61)

These villains—Johnny Quick, Superwoman, Owlman, Power Ring, and Ultraman—are clear variations of heroes who appear on both Earth-One and Earth-Two (the Flash, Wonder Woman, Batman, Green Lantern, and Superman, respectively). As one might suspect, the Crime Syndicate becomes aware of their Earth-One counterparts and wishes to battle them. After transporting the heroes of Earth-One to Earth-Three in order to defeat them, the Syndicate then sets its eyes on Earth-Two, but the JLA is able to warn the Justice Society about this impending attack. Ultimately, the two teams overcome the villains of Earth-Three and imprison them in between dimensions.

By introducing the Crime Syndicate as an "evil Justice League" in this storyline, in a world where everything is opposite to Earth-One, Fox for the first time really starts exploring the wider concept of the multiverse. Not only was he able to reintroduce older characters, but he could also create new ones. For example, two years later, in *Justice League of America* #46's "Crisis Between Earth-One and Earth-Two!" he introduced the Anti-Matter Man, an incredibly powerful entity from an alternate antimatter universe. Later still, in 1968's *Justice League of America* #64, he completely reinvented an old superhero parody, the Red Tornado, as a superpowered android who joins the JSA only to try to destroy them from within. At the same time, he wasn't done creating new Earths either; in 1968's *The Flash* #170, Barry Allen accidentally travels to an Earth with no superheroes, where his own exploits are just comic book stories. This, we find out, is our *own* Earth, known as Earth-Prime, and Julius Schwartz himself guest stars and helps Barry figure out how to return home.[6]

Fox was not the only creator slowly building up the multiverse, though. Outside of the annual JLA/JSA team-ups, individual heroes would cross dimensions to team up with each other, as in 1965's "Secret Origin of the Guardians!" in *Green Lantern* #40, written by John Broome. This issue not only brought together the magically powered Green Lantern of Earth-Two (Alan Scott) with the science-based "space cop" Green Lantern of Earth-One (Hal Jordan), but it also finally provided the origin story of the latter's cosmic overseers, a race of little blue men called the Guardians of the Universe. This issue would become crucial to the DC Multiverse in that it first reveals the nigh-mythological origin story of a rogue Guardian named Krona who created a device to look back at the dawn of the universe. The image that he sees there—a hand made out of star-stuff, gripping a swirling galaxy, a suitably cosmic picture from master artist Gil Kane—would become a central metaphor for the origins of the DC Multiverse, as we shall see. By daring to observe this seminal moment, Krona unwittingly unleashes evil throughout the universe for eternity. As we would later learn, he also, in this instant, actually *created* the multiverse.

Other writers eventually followed Fox as the regular scripters of *Justice League of America*, and thus as the creators behind the annual team-up with the Justice Society. While Fox, by the end of his tenure, was more interested in creating and reinvigorating older characters, these new writers would soon get to work building out the multiverse even further in these cross-dimensional capers. For example, 1973's "Crisis on Earth-X!" running through issues #107 and #108 of *Justice League of America*, brought members of both teams of heroes to a newly discovered dimension where the Nazis actually won World War II. However, this world has superheroes too, in the form of the Freedom Fighters, an underground resistance strike force led by Uncle Sam, the physical embodiment of the American fighting spirit.

The mastermind of this storyline, writer Len Wein, used it to achieve multiple goals. First, he was able to bring into DC continuity a series of heroes who had originally been part of the now defunct Quality Comics' stable of characters, the rights to which DC Comics had purchased. He also, as scholar Peter W. Lee points out, played into the sentimental nostalgia of the early 1970s (a turbulent period in American history) for the perceived "Good War" that had been

World War II. Lee argues that Wein deliberately intended to explore American disenchantment with overseas adventurism in Vietnam by positing the U.S. war machine as the *Nazis* of Earth-X. According to Lee, Wein allegorized a foolish U.S. foreign policy built upon perpetuating a military bureaucracy:

> The mythos—a blind faith in the military to succeed through overwhelming technical might—had become a perpetuating cycle. For the Nazis, the master race could only achieve victory if it subjugated all remaining resistance. For the world of the readers, the fallout from the 1970s disenchantment was the catalyst that led to Len Wein penning this adventure in the first place.

(75)

We thus see here another important aspect of the multiverse-as-storytelling-engine—the ability to create new worlds that could serve more directly as metaphors for the contemporary world. Comics had evolved a lot throughout the 1960s, taking on contemporary issues, and Wein belonged to a more modern generation of writers than Gardner Fox had. He was interested not just in escapist stories, but in making a point to his readers about the society and politics of the world around them. Earth-X allowed him to do just that.

Nor would Earth-X be the last world used to that purpose. In 1976's "Crisis on Earth-S!" (running through *Justice League of America* #135–137), writers E. Nelson Bridwell and Martin Pasko introduced Earth-S, home to the characters DC had purchased from the defunct publisher Fawcett Comics, including the popular Captain Marvel (the hero with the mind of a boy in the body of a superpowered man). Bridwell and Pasko didn't just reintroduce these characters, but also used the story as an opportunity to comment on the childlike innocence of the old Captain Marvel stories compared to the more serious, socially aware stories of the present, as embodied by a barely averted clash between the Captain and a maniacally enraged Superman of Earth-One. By this point, both comics storytelling and the multiverse had evolved to the point where they could create metaphors about real-world issues within these multidimensional crossovers.

The Multiverse in Full Bloom

Future JLA/JSA team-ups would be just as cosmically expansive, not only exploring other dimensions, but also other worlds and time periods, thus bringing into continuity many of the characters from DC's western and war titles, allowing the JLA to meet the heroic Legion of Superheroes from DC's distant future, and folding master writer/artist Jack Kirby's "Fourth World" continuity into the main DC Universe. By 1982, the annual meeting traveled through time, brought in both Earth-Prime and the evil Crime Syndicate, and even expanded beyond the pages of just *Justice League of America*, crossing over into the pages of *All-Star Squadron*, a series set entirely on Earth-Two.

Writer Gerry Conway had previously revived the Justice Society in their own ongoing series that ran in the late 1970s in *All Star Comics* and *Adventure Comics*. These stories were set in the present day on Earth-Two, featuring an aged Justice Society mentoring younger heroes. It introduced characters such as Power Girl (Superman's cousin and ostensibly the Earth-Two version of Supergirl) and the Huntress (the grown-up daughter of Batman and Catwoman), and even portrayed the death of Batman, in another example of how the multiplicity of the multiverse enables emotionally resonant stories that would never be allowed in the "main" continuity.

All-Star Squadron, on the other hand, took place in the 1930s, at the outset of America's entrance into World War II (the very first storyline, in fact, concerns the attack on Pearl Harbor, in order to explain why the Earth-Two heroes were unable to prevent that tragic attack). The brainchild of writer Roy Thomas, *All-Star Squadron* featured not just the Justice Society, but *all* of DC's heroes from the "Golden Age," including those later purchased from other publishers, in stories that attempted to recreate and rationalize some of the more convoluted and naive ideas of those early comic books. The title would prove to be such a success that it spawned something of a spin-off, *Infinity, Inc.*, a book set in the present day of Earth-Two. However, rather than just showing older duplicates of the main Earth-One heroes, *Infinity, Inc.*

featured the sons and daughters of the original JSA as they created their own superhero team.

For many years—including in the crossover with *Justice League of America*—Thomas was essentially given free reign as the shepherd of Earth-Two, in charge of both its history and its future. In his stories, he chose to downplay the multiplicity angle (likely because he knew that readers were less interested in slightly different versions of characters already starring in their own books *and* appearing in *Justice League of America*), and focus instead on the historical ties to DC's past in *All-Star Squadron* and the legacy aspect of a new generation of heroes in *Infinity, Inc.* Whereas the "main" Superman, Batman, Wonder Woman, et al. of Earth-One were prevented by DC editorial from ever aging, getting married, having children, or dying (Earth-One continuity at DC was very conservative, so as to not meddle with the formula that had kept the characters successful for so many decades), on Earth-Two Thomas was able to show what it would be like if real, generational change actually happened, a novel idea in superhero stories at the time.

As literary scholar Terrence R. Wandtke explains, the entire Earth-Two concept playfully "breaks from Aristotle's insistence that stories fool the audience into thinking they've experienced reality . . . [and] ultimately makes variation more important than primacy, authenticity, and even originality" (144). More specifically, he notes that:

> Earth-2 allowed writers to explore certain facets of these characters that, at the time, could never be explored within the regular series of adventures of these . . . heroes (such as Superman marrying Lois Lane and Batman retiring, thus allowing his sidekick Robin to take center stage). As readers could look back and forth between the end of Superman's story on Earth-2 and the on-going stories of the younger Superman on Earth-1 with no real cognitive dissonance, readers could also experience almost unending variation as the multiverse expanded; the love of variation seemed to feed itself and further encourage variation as an end in itself.
>
> (145)

Wandtke then goes on to argue that:

> the pseudo-science of the multiverse is largely an excuse for a certain kind of storytelling. The logos of hard science serves as an excuse to return to the mythos of superhero variation, and the either/or paradigm of scientific objectivity is forsaken for a multiverse of possibilities that address the current culture.
>
> (145–146)

While Wandtke is interested in the multiplicity/possibility of the multiverse in order to argue for the role of orality as a central aspect of superhero storytelling, he points to something vitally important about these early decades of the DC Multiverse, and a theme as important to stories about the multiverse as legacy and multiplicity are—the playfulness of it all. Fox, Thomas, and numerous other creators who added to the multiverse used those stories as an opportunity to tell big, bold, cosmic stories with exciting visuals featuring dozens of heroes and villains in action. They seized upon the opportunity to do new, exciting things with characters such as Superman and Batman who were otherwise stuck in an eternal present where nothing ever changes beyond the surface trappings. They created whole worlds through which to explore intriguing concepts, such as Earth-Prime and Earth-X, while at the same time working to make those concepts meaningful to the characters that readers regularly followed.

For a comic book publisher concerned primarily with putting out a line of monthly titles, this playfulness was a welcome trait, and one that proved financially successful if we are to gauge by the dedication to an annual JLA/JSA team-up. By the mid-1980s, though, DC Comics was more than just a publisher; it was the herald of valuable intellectual property that was being translated into movies, TVs, games, and merchandise. Though the multiverse might make sense to longtime readers, many executives and editors at the company feared that, for example, viewers of the Richard Donner 1978 *Superman* movie who wanted to read the comics that inspired the films would be confused by multiple versions of the same character, one of whom was graying at the temples and married and another of whom was young and single.

As these DC Comics stakeholders became more concerned with shepherding a singular, cohesive universe that could both sell comic books and be spun off into other lucrative endeavors—in short, as they came to think of the DC Universe as a vital and fecund imaginary world—they realized that something had to be done about the multiverse.

Notes

1 Though many scholars and historians rightly point to a rich prehistory of superheroes, ranging from the gods and goddesses of world mythology to the heroes of epics such as *Gilgamesh* and *Beowulf*, the character of Superman was the first real "superhero" in our modern conception of the term. See Coogan, among many other sources,

2 Though Levitz refers to the series as *Justice Society of America*, that was just the name of the team; the book in which they appeared was *All-Star Comics*.

3 For a general history of this era in the comic book industry, see Jones and Wright.

4 See Jones, Wright, and Gilbert.

5 Though "Flash of Two Worlds!" is widely considered the first appearance of the DC Multiverse, an article from the website *Comic Book Resources* notes that in 1953's *Wonder Woman* #59, the title character "travels to a 'mirror' world that exists in parallel to our own. There she meets her alternate self, called Tara Terruna, and this world—later designated Earth 59—was almost identical to Wonder Woman's. While the multiverse will be expanded on and explored in more depth in later comics, this is where the construct first took shape" (Lune).

6 Earth-Prime would be used, at first, mostly for humorous stories wherein DC's writers transposed themselves into their own comic books, but later versions would be used for darker and more explicit metaphors about the creators and readers on "our" Earth.

References

Coogan, Peter. *Superhero: The Secret Origin of a Genre*. Austin, TX: MonkeyBrain Books, 2006.

Fox, Gardner, writer, Carmine Infantino, penciller, and Julius Schwartz, editor, et al. "Flash of Two Worlds!" *Flash* 123. Reprinted in *Crisis on Multiple Earths: The Team-Ups*, edited by Robert Greenberger. New York: DC Comics, 2005.

Fox, Gardner, writer, Carmine Infantino, penciller, and Julius Schwartz, editor, et al. "Vengeance of the Immortal Villain!" *Flash* 137. Reprinted in *Crisis on Multiple Earths: The Team-Ups*, edited by Robert Greenberger. New York: DC Comics, 2005.

Fox, Gardner, writer, Mike Sekowsky, penciller, and Julius Schwartz, editor, et al. "Crisis on Earth-One!" *Justice League of America* 21. Reprinted in *Crisis on Multiple Earths*, edited by Nick J. Napolitano. New York: DC Comics, 2002.

Fox, Gardner, writer, Mike Sekowsky, penciller, and Julius Schwartz, editor, et al. "Crisis on Earth-Two!" *Justice League of America* 22. Reprinted in *Crisis on Multiple Earths*, edited by Nick J. Napolitano. New York: DC Comics, 2002.

Fox, Gardner, writer, Mike Sekowsky, penciller, and Julius Schwartz, editor, et al. "Crisis on Earth-Three!" *Justice League of America* 29. Reprinted in *Crisis on Multiple Earths*, edited by Nick J. Napolitano. New York: DC Comics, 2002.

Gilbert, James. *A Cycle of Outrage: America's Reaction to the Juvenile Delinquent in the 1950s*. New York: Oxford University Press, 1986.

Jones, Gerard. *Men of Tomorrow: Geeks, Gangsters and the Birth of the Comic Book*. New York: Basic Books, 2004.

Lee, Peter W. "A Crisis of Infinite Dearth: Winning Vietnam via the Never-Ending War on Earth-X." In *The Ages of the Justice League: Essays on America's Greatest Superheroes in Changing Times*, edited by Joseph J. Darowski. Jefferson, NC: McFarland & Company, 2017.

Levitz, Paul. *75 Years of DC Comics: The Art of Modern Mythmaking*. Cologne, Germany: Taschen, 2010.

Lune, Matt. "The DC Multiverse: 15 Facts to Know (Before It Hits the Movies)." *Comic Book Resources*. Last modified September 23, 2017. www.cbr.com/the-dc-multiverse-important-facts/.

Ndalianis, Angela. "Enter the Aleph: Superhero Worlds and Hypertime Realities." In *The Contemporary Comic Book Superhero*, edited by Angela Ndalianis. New York: Routledge, 2009.

Waid, Mark. "1 & 2 = Crisis." In *Crisis on Multiple Earths*, edited by Nick J. Napolitano. New York: DC Comics, 2002.

Wandtke, Terrence R. *The Meaning of Superhero Comics*. Jefferson, NC: McFarland & Company, 2012.

Wright, Bradford W. *Comic Book Nation: The Transformation of Youth Culture in America*. Baltimore, MD: Johns Hopkins University Press, 2001.

2 The Multiverse in Crisis

The first phase of the DC Multiverse was one of expansion and exploration, a combination of new characters and worlds welded together with older ideas to create one overarching imaginary world out of what had been several independent publishers' lineups of heroes and villains. It was also a widely disconnected process, one that evolved haphazardly without any kind of overarching creative or editorial stewardship. Each new addition to the multiverse came independently, rather than as part of a larger plan heading towards some kind of narrative goal, and instead focused on the new concept or idea that was being introduced in each individual story. It was, in short, a period of expansion.

The second phase of the multiverse, which began with 1985's 12-issue *Crisis on Infinite Earths* crossover event, was a period of contraction and limitation. It was only in 2018, with the miniseries *Dark Knights: Metal*, that this second phase reached its endpoint as the DC Multiverse once again entered a period where the energetic potential of creative possibility overcame editorial squeamishness that favored simplicity. As this chapter will show, the second phase of the multiverse put that imaginary world into a cyclical series of crises that placed the key tenants of the multiverse—multiplicity and legacy—directly at their center.

Crisis on Infinite Earths

Crisis on Infinite Earths (often shortened to just *Crisis*) was in many ways the prototypical comic book crossover, one that publishers are still emulating to this day with greater or lesser degrees of success. For better or worse, it was also perhaps the crossover series with the single most far-reaching impact on its universe (or, in this case, multiverse), and was a crucial moment not just in the history of DC Comics' imaginary world, but also in the history of DC Comics as a company. According to Paul Levitz (who was a creative executive at DC Comics at the time):

> To celebrate DC's 50th anniversary in 1985, the company decided to destroy the Earths. Since Julie Schwartz and Gardner Fox introduced the concept of multiple, parallel Earths, it had been one of the most intriguing aspects of DC mythology—but also arguably one of the most confusing. Writer-editor Gerry Conway had first proposed collapsing the Earths into one in the late 1970s, but in the mid-1980s it seemed like an important step to take in the increased competition with Marvel and its then-simpler continuity.
>
> (559–560)

In practice, what this meant was that DC Comics' imaginary world was to go from an expansive multiverse to a single, cohesive universe.

The very first page of the first issue of *Crisis* (titled "The Summoning!") even implies that the multiverse was never meant to be. A series of captions penned by writer Marv Wolfman run alongside, and overlay, artist George Pérez's representation of the Big Bang. The captions read:

> In the beginning there was only one, a single black infinitude . . . so cold and dark for so very long . . . that even the burning light was imperceptible. But the light grew, and the infinitude shuddered . . . and the darkness finally . . . screamed, as much in pain as in relief. For in that instant a multiverse was born. A multiverse of worlds vibrating and replicating . . . and a multiverse that should have been one, became many.
>
> (11)

In the final panel of the page, Pérez shows a series of Earths that have been birthed by this explosive event, with each Earth slightly overlapping the one next to it. This image—multiple Earths in a row, overlapping each other like Venn diagrams—would come to be a defining image of the DC Multiverse, and a visual shorthand that would be employed throughout the second phase of the multiverse.[1]

From that first page, *Crisis* #1 segues into the destruction of two different Earths by unstoppable walls of white antimatter—first an Earth that is unnamed and appears to have no superheroes, and then Earth-Three, home of the Crime Syndicate. It seems to be no coincidence that Wolfman and Pérez open their story with the destruction of the very first Earth intentionally added to the multiverse two decades prior (as opposed to Earth-One and Earth-Two, which were both preexisting worlds that Gardner Fox and Julius Schwartz had simply slapped a name onto). If *Crisis* was to be the unraveling and undoing of the multiverse, it made sense for it to start where the multiverse itself had (metatextually) begun its expansion.

As the story progresses, we learn that a cosmic being known as the Monitor is attempting to prevent the destruction of the multiverse at the hands of his opposite number from an antimatter universe, an evil being known as the Anti-Monitor. As the Monitor himself explains in issue #4 ("And Thus Shall the World DIE!"), reiterating the opening captions, "The universe was split apart at the dawn of time . . . each world weaker than the whole it was meant to be" (114–115). The destructive wave of antimatter overcoming the multiverse also plays off of Gardner Fox's original theory of the multiverse, that all the Earths are in the same place at the same time, just vibrating at different frequencies. The Monitor, with his death at the hands of his assistant, Harbinger (who has been temporarily corrupted by the Anti-Monitor), is able to use his cosmic energies to place the universes that have not been destroyed by the antimatter into a "netherverse," but in a video message revealed in issue #5 ("Worlds in Limbo") he warns that "The vibrations which separate the universes are slowing down . . . the universes are merging . . . and when they occupy the same space at the same time . . . they will destroy each other!" (125).

In order to combat this threat, the Monitor and Harbinger recruit heroes and villains from throughout the multiverse, and especially from Earth-One and Earth-Two. The entire miniseries, even as it sets about to destroy the multiplicity of the imaginary world of DC Comics, is an ode to that multiplicity, with multiple versions of various characters appearing throughout. Wolfman and Pérez even take the time to introduce a brand-new dimension that is home to the characters from defunct publisher Charlton, bringing them into the fold of the DC Multiverse. Thus, *Crisis* is a love letter to the very multiverse it works so hard to destroy.

In fact, it is within *Crisis* that the multiverse's origin is provided for the first time. This origin ties back to an earlier story of the multiverse, the encounter between the Green Lanterns of Earth-One and Earth-Two in 1965's *Green Lantern* #40. In *Crisis* #7 ("Beyond the Silent Night"), we learn that when rogue Guardian of the Universe Krona looked back to the dawn of time and saw the image of a giant hand holding a cluster of stars, he not only released evil into the universe for the first time, but that also:

> The universe shuddered . . . and the evil antimatter universe was formed. But more than that—the single universe was replicated. What was one became many. At that moment was born both the antimatter universe and the multiverse. The Earth . . . and all the planets were duplicated.
>
> (183)

Thus, the multiverse was the unintentional side effect of a cosmic accident, and its multiplicity and diversity are what make it weak to attacks from the antimatter universe (despite, ironically, *Crisis*'s own reveling in that multiplicity).

After the assembled heroes of the remaining Earths foil several of the Anti-Monitor's plans (resulting in a few noble sacrifices, including that of Barry Allen, the character most associated with the multiverse and with DC's "Silver Age"), the villain travels back to the dawn of time in order to destroy the multiverse before it is ever born. The heroes follow him back and—with the aid of the godlike hero/angel of vengeance called the Spectre—combat his scheme. This battle rages at the end of issue #10 ("Death at the Dawn of Time!"), which concludes with an image of the Spectre literally shattering to pieces, only blank, white space—the blank whiteness of the empty page—left underneath. The captions overlaying this shattered imagery note that the Spectre:

> sees worlds that have never existed and never will! He sees shapes and colors and patterns and concepts undreamt of even by his master! And the Spectre screams again! And the universe explodes around him. And, from the dawn of creation . . . comes death . . . It is the end of all that was.
>
> (295)

The very first page of the next issue (fittingly titled "Aftershock"), however, shows us what comes after "all that was" has ended:

> In the beginning there were many, a multiversal infinitude . . . so cold and dark for so very long . . . that even the burning light was imperceptible. But then the light grew, and the multiverse shuddered . . . and the darkness screamed as much in pain as in relief. For in that instant a universe was born. A universe with many worlds orbiting burning suns. A universe reborn at the dawn of time. What had been many became one.
>
> (297)

These words are in captions that run across a series of four panels that very nearly mirror the first page of *Crisis* #1, save that the final panel, rather than showing several overlapping Earths, only shows a singular Earth in a single universe.

The remaining two issues of *Crisis* deal with the fallout of this, including one final knockdown, drag-out fight with the Anti-Monitor and his army of destructive shadow demons. The heroes reassemble and learn that the DC Multiverse has been reborn as the singular DC Universe, which essentially resembles Earth-One with characters from the other Earths transposed to it. Exactly how the backstories of these characters have changed (or not) is very confusing, both for the characters in the story, the creators working at DC Comics at the time, and the readers, but over time those continuity issues came to more or less settle into a unified post-*Crisis* history of the DC Universe.

Wolfman and Pérez even provided an escape route to the Superman of Earth-Two, the original superhero who first appeared in *Action Comics* #1, along with his wife Lois; the young son of Lex Luthor from Earth-Three; and the Superboy from Earth-Prime (the only superhero from that universe, who had been created as a part of *Crisis*). This allows for a somewhat more sentimental goodbye to those characters, serving as stand-ins for the multiplicity and expansive creativity of the multiverse. The young Alexander Luthor, as he transports them all to some kind of undefined heaven-like realm at the end of *Crisis* #12 ("Final Crisis"), explains:

> I knew how the universe would be reborn . . . I knew the consequences. And I could not let *you*, of all the heroes, suffer in that loss. . . . Where we go now there will be no fear . . . only peace . . . ever-lasting peace.
>
> (360)

As we shall see, though, that peace was ultimately not to be everlasting.

The entire miniseries wraps up in the twelfth and final issue with a monologue from Harbinger, noting how the universe has changed in the wake of its rebirth:

> From death comes life, and each life brings hope for a brighter, happier future. With the end of the multiverse and the beginning of the new Earth, there now is one consistent past. . . . We should never forget the past, but we should always look to the future . . . because that's where we're going to spend the rest of our lives. I don't know about you guys, but I can't wait to see what tomorrow will bring.
>
> (362–363)

With that, the DC Multiverse officially became the DC Universe.

In practice, though, creating this singular DC Universe meant losing much of the expansive, anarchic charm that had defined the DC Multiverse, including the "anything can happen" sensibility of the annual JLA/JSA crossovers where each year's story attempted to somehow top the last. Rather, as comics blogger Andrew Hickey points out, the impulse to imply rigid order here is so counter to that anarchic charm that it borders on fascism:

> [D]iversity is weakness, and unity is strength. There should be only one of each thing, and any deviation from the central version of something should be destroyed. . . . [The] need for completion and closure, and disapproval of deviation from that, is something that is compatible with fascism, and that is reflected structurally in the basis of *Crisis on Infinite Earths*. There's a real tension here, in fact—the whole story, all the time, celebrates the diversity of the DC Multiverse . . . and shows all the massive potential the characters and situations have, while simultaneously telling us these things aren't good like you think, but bad really, and need to be destroyed in order to have a cleaner storytelling universe.

Hickey also makes the crucial point that this impetus is:

> fundamentally based on a false premise, which is that the concept of a multiverse is too complicated. This is clearly nonsense—I remember reading, several years before I properly got into comics, several random issues of DC comics involving the Earth-One and Earth-Two versions of heroes teaming up. I couldn't have been more than eight, but I found nothing confusing in this. . . . [T]he vast majority of fans will not have been confused, but those small number who were would be vocal about it. As that small number were the ones that the editors were hearing from—well, that causes problems when you're trying to tailor stuff to the fans.

Though obviously this is just one critic's opinion, based on his own anecdotal evidence, it is reiterated more charitably by scholar Julian Darius:

> To hardcore fans who didn't need footnotes explaining past stories, DC's system of multiple Earths could be a great narrative wonder, joyous in its complexity and permutations. But it wasn't

exactly inviting to new readers. And it could confuse even DC's writers and editors. At some point, complexity began turning to chaos and became perceived as a mess that needed fixing.

(172)

However, there were many readers and fans of DC Comics who felt that the "narrative wonder" was more important than being new-reader-friendly. Two decades later, it was those kinds of readers who had grown up to become professional comic book writers themselves, and were now at the helm of DC's future.

Infinite Crisis and *52*

One such writer was Geoff Johns, who had grown up a major fan of DC Comics and rapidly rose in popularity with fans and critics alike upon breaking into the industry in 2000. By 2005, he was the company's biggest draw as a writer, and had shown with long runs on *The Flash* and *JSA* (a modern-day reinvention of the Justice Society) that he was particularly adept at turning complex continuity into a compelling, emotionally resonant story rather than just a complicated impediment to storytelling. It wasn't entirely surprising, then, that he was given the reigns of the seven-issue series *Infinite Crisis*, which celebrated the twentieth anniversary of *Crisis on Infinite Earths* by bringing back the four characters who survived the original *Crisis*, and thus remembered the multiverse (Superman and Lois Lane of Earth-Two, Alexander Luthor of Earth-Three, and Superboy of Earth-Prime), to show how they reacted to a DC Universe that had gone through the "grim and gritty" period of comics in the 1980s and 1990s and was now a much darker place to live than the multiverse had ever been.

As he hammers his way out of the crystalline "heaven" they have been confined to for two decades (a heaven that we find out was more of a purgatory, where they could only watch helplessly as the events of the DC Universe unfolded), the Earth-Two Superman complains at the end of *Infinite Crisis* #1, "We've given them a gift they've thrown away. We sacrificed everything for them" (39). Just as the first *Crisis* had been a commentary on the complexity of the multiverse, and how it was a liability to telling the kinds of more streamlined, mature, and "realistic" comic book stories that came into vogue in the mid-1980s, *Infinite Crisis* sets out as a repudiation of that conceit, embodied by the returned characters' desire to go back to a simpler time less infested with dark storytelling. In issue #2, the Earth-Two Superman explains:

> When the universe was reborn, Earth-One became the primary world. The scraps of the remaining worlds were folded into it. But I finally realize—we saved the wrong Earth. . . . This corrupted and darkened Earth must be forgotten as ours was . . . so that the *right* Earth can return.
>
> (72)

However, as the series progresses, we learn that Alexander Luthor has been manipulating both Superman and Superboy-Prime in order to gain the power needed to remake the DC Universe into what he perceives as "the perfect Earth," *not* to restore Earth-Two. Luthor uses a device created from the Anti-Monitor's shattered armor, and powered by several characters originally from different Earths, in order to bring back the multiverse. He manipulates the energies unleashed by his machine with his own two hands, recreating the imagery from the original *Crisis* of a starry hand holding a galaxy of stars. When the multiple Earths return, they overlap one another in the sky, also reviving imagery from the original *Crisis*. These echoes are intentional, placed there by Johns and the team of artists he is working with (primarily penciller Phil Jimenez, whose detailed style is heavily influenced by Pérez) in order to indicate that, after 20 years of a singular DC Universe, the DC Multiverse was experiencing a new origin point.

The heroes of the DC Universe manage to destroy Luther's tower, however, foiling his plans. What results is not a new multiverse, but rather "New Earth," which is the same post-*Crisis* DC Universe with a few changes to continuity. However, the point of *Infinite Crisis* was not, specifically, to revive the multiverse, but rather to make the case that the modern incarnations of the DC heroes are every bit as idyllic and heroic as they were in the years before *Crisis on Infinite Earths*, with the Superman of Earth-Two sacrificing himself in order to save this post-*Crisis* universe once he sees its value. As Julian Darius puts it, "*Infinite Crisis* showed itself a fusion of past and present, venerating DC's history while also flowing out of more recent tastes and developments" (205).

Rather than ending with the return of the multiverse, the focus here is on the heroes of this New Earth, who have proven their mettle and come together after several years' worth of infighting prior to *Infinite Crisis*. In the final issue, #7, New Earth's Superman tells Batman and Wonder Woman, "I know we'll always have our differences, but at the end of the day we all want the same thing. Justice. When Earth needs us standing together again, we find a way. No matter what" (244–245).

With the value of New Earth, of DC's main continuity, thus reiterated by *Infinite Crisis*, the miniseries' follow-up, called *52* (a 52-issue weekly series co-written by Geoff Johns along with fellow writers Grant Morrison, Mark Waid, and Greg Rucka), could take the next step forward and finally bring back the multiverse. In the series' final issue, "A Year in the Life," time-traveling heroes Rip Hunter and Booster Gold return to the climax of *Infinite Crisis* and discover what should be a familiar image to readers—a series of Earths floating in a cosmic void, reminiscent of the visualization of the multiverse in both *Crisis on Infinite Earths* and *Infinite Crisis*. Hunter, an experienced time traveler, tells Booster, "We're witnessing the birth of the new multiverse. Each parallel Earth an exact copy of ours in every way" (283). He explains that when Alexander Luthor's tower had been destroyed in *Infinite Crisis*:

> The broken Earths collapsed back together, combining historical remnants to form one new Earth—one far too small to contain the energy within it. In a cosmic act of self-preservation, as you just saw, it began replicating. Unknown to anyone save myself, a new multiverse was born in the wake of this crisis. 52 identical earths in 52 identical cosmos.
>
> (284–285)

However, the birth of the new multiverse in *52* was not to be contained merely to identical copies; it also saw a return to the multiplicity and diversity of the original multiverse. The climax of *52* features Hunter and Booster fighting against Mr. Mind, a hyper-intelligent, super-evolved worm that is attempting to feed off the energies of the 52 identical Earths. In the process, as Hunter explains, "He's eating years and events from [each] universe's history. . . . He's altering [each] Earth with every bite he takes. With every flap of his wings" (290). As a result, the 52 Earths all become uniquely differentiated, creating new, updated versions of worlds from the classic multiverse such as the Justice Society's Earth-Two, the Crime Syndicate's Earth-Three, the Charlton characters' Earth-Four, the Freedom Fighters' Earth-X (now known as Earth-Ten), and Captain Marvel's Earth-S (now Earth-Five). We also see several new dimensions, such as Earth-22, apparently home to the events of the originally out-of-continuity apocalyptic miniseries *Kingdom Come*, and Earth-50, home to the characters from Wildstorm, a publishing imprint that DC had purchased some years prior.

Right off the bat, then, the new multiverse created in *Infinite Crisis* and *52* reflects the traditions of the original multiverse. We see the legacy of reinvented worlds and characters revived among a multiplicity of different versions of characters, all while integrating previously separate stories and characters into the larger imaginary world of the DC Multiverse. As co-writer Mark Waid notes, this was deliberate and intentional:

> When it came time to map the alternate Earths, we elected to invent new ones rather than simply reestablish familiar ones from old DC comics. That said, many are designed to deliberately resemble DC worlds of yore, such as Earth-22 (Home of the KINGDOM COME miniseries) and Earth-5 (formerly 'Earth-S,' the 'S' standing for 'Shazam').
>
> (321)

Within the story, though, Booster Gold worries that the diversity of this new multiverse means the heroes have failed, and broken all of reality. Rip Hunter responds:

> Broken or opened? Look around you, Booster. There's so much more happening out there than we could ever have imagined. That's not "broken." That's the way things should be. Welcome to a multiverse of possibility, Booster. Welcome home.
>
> (311–313)

According to Waid, the metaphor of homecoming here, as well as the excitement over new creative possibility, is also intentional:

> "Welcome home" is my favorite line in the entire series. "Home," both to us as writers and to our characters, is not a constriction of rules and regulations in which only one "definitive" interpretation of the DC heroes can exist and everything not currently in vogue is "wrong"; it's a multiverse of possibility where absolutely anything can happen and where imagination has no limits. From the time a caveman told the first bedtime story to today, no good fiction ever came out of worrying first and foremost whether its events fit into "continuity."
>
> (321)

Despite Waid's poetic musings, though, much of the remainder of this second phase of the DC Multiverse *would* consist of stories attempting to quantify and chart the continuity of these 52 Earths.

Final Crisis

From the outset of this new multiverse, with the declarative notion that there are only 52 Earths, DC Comics was attempting to return to the creative possibility of the multiverse without risking the infinite expansiveness of the original multiverse. This, then, was a *contained* multiverse, as opposed to the *expansive* multiverse of the first phase. Strangely, though, the task of charting the new multiverse would fall largely to one of the most uncontained writers in comic books—fan-favorite British writer Grant Morrison, whose blend of pop sensibility and large-scale cosmic storytelling led to comics that were both sales successes and critical darlings.

His first big story about the new multiverse, though, titled *Final Crisis* (and intended to be the final story in the "trilogy" begun with *Crisis on Infinite Earths* and *Infinite Crisis*), was caught between these two imperatives, trying to create a sales blockbuster that was also filled with heady concepts, ultimately meeting somewhere in the middle in a relatively unsatisfying fusion. It was also hampered by a yearlong, weekly prelude miniseries, *Countdown to Final Crisis*, which spent so much time exploring the multiverse in such a haphazard manner that the bloom was already well off the rose by the time the first issue of *Final Crisis* even came out.

Though the multiverse of 52 Earths certainly plays a role in *Final Crisis*, the story itself focuses much more on the ultimate battle between good (represented by the DC heroes) and evil (represented by the evil "New God" Darkseid, who had by this time become the most powerful villain at DC Comics, with the possible exception of the Anti-Monitor), and how the heroes can overcome the odds and ultimately succeed even after they have seemingly lost. However, a subplot revolves around the revived "Multiversal Monitors," 52 variants of the original Monitor from *Crisis on Infinite Earths*,[2] and the "Orrery of Worlds" that they protect. Primary *Final Crisis* artist J.G. Jones represents this Orrery in *Final Crisis* #1 ("D.O.A.: The GOD of WAR") as a kind of immense glass tube framed with intricate metalwork, within which the 52 Earths are nested like a funnel, with Earth-Zero (the new name for the "New Earth" created at the end of *Infinite Crisis*, which the Monitors call "the foundation stone of all existence" [25]) at the very bottom.

The multiverse takes center stage in the two-issue spin-off series *Final Crisis: Superman Beyond* by Morrison and penciller Doug Mahnke. The story features a female Monitor named Zillo Valla gathering together multiple versions of Superman from across the multiverse in order to save the world of the Monitors, which has come under threat from a fallen, corrupted, dark Monitor named Mandrakk. Zillo Valla's ship is attacked, and the Supermen end up stranded in limbo, a dimension beyond the 52 universes that is home to all of the characters who have been lost and forgotten over the course of DC Comics' history.[3] There, they find a book with "an infinite number of pages, all occupying the same space" (21), meaning that it contains the text of everything ever written. Upon reading the book using his super-vision, Superman is granted a look into the revised origin of the multiverse, one that is even more cosmic and metatextual than the origin first revealed in *Crisis on Infinite Earths*.

Morrison's writing is often deliberately vague and elliptical, focusing as much on energy, bombast, and sentiment as on clearing up specific issues of continuity, and as a result his origin of the Monitors and the multiverse is not entirely clear nor easy to relate. The confusion is increased by Mahnke's art in this segment of *Superman Beyond* #1, which focuses on psychedelic, iconic imagery rather than clear explication of the ambiguous captions. As Superman attempts to explain, he learns that prior to the birth of the multiverse, all that existed was "Some kind of abstract, infinite intelligence, the biggest life form I've ever encountered. A conscious, living void! With our entire multiverse growing inside it" (23). As represented by a blank white panel, this "void" is the white page itself.

The multiverse, then, is composed of the stories put down upon the page by creators ranging from Gardner Fox and Marv Wolfman to Geoff Johns and Morrison himself. This origin story is deliberately metatextual, a favorite trope of Morrison, and poetically ties together the in-story cosmology of the multiverse with the very act of creating a comic book, of sketching stories and images down on previously blank paper. It is also a love letter to those stories, as Superman—the ur-superhero, representative of the creative magic of the entire multiverse—is deliberately chosen to combat Mandrakk, a cosmic vampire who wishes to feed upon a multiverse that he sees as an infection of story and emotion upon the pristine, blank page. Morrison, though, argues that these stories inspire us, and that the creative possibilities of the multiverse are more valuable than the blank nothingness Mandrakk craves. As Superman battles Mandrakk in *Superman Beyond* #2, Zillo Valla looks on and proclaims that "deep within the germ-worlds, I found a better story; one created to be unstoppable, indestructible! The story of a child rocketed to Earth from a doomed planet . . ." (21). Superman, here representing the entire multiverse, is too creative and powerful of an idea—and an ideal—to be stopped.

In the final issue of *Final Crisis* ("New Heaven, New Earth"), in the grand tradition of stories about the multiverse, Morrison introduces us to a new Earth—this one featuring an African-American Superman who, in his secret identity, is President of the United States (a clear reference to the then-recent election of Barack Obama as president, something seen by many—Morrison included—as a sign of hope and change after several dark years post-9/11). While adding new worlds and focusing on new possibilities, though, Morrison is also closing off old narrative lines. The Monitors' world is returned to the blank white page of the "overmind" by one of their own, Nix Uotan, who has become the most powerful of them all during the course of the story. As Uotan explains, shortly before beginning the destruction of their world, "We almost destroyed this beautiful living thing in our midst. This multiverse of life deserves its freedom from our interference. Make your peace" (34). Uotan himself, though, remains to watch over the multiverse and to help its citizens defend themselves from threats. He wakes up, in a human body on Earth Zero, and hears a news report saying, "You've just joined WGBS on a beautiful day in Metropolis. With more on those newly discovered parallel worlds and how they could change our lives forever! This is one story that's only just beginning" (35). As the final line of dialogue in the series, this also serves as *Final Crisis*'s mission statement—the story continues, even after the "final" crisis faced by DC's heroes, and that story will involve a revitalized and rejuvenated multiverse.

Convergence **and** *Multiversity*

The multiverse of 52 Earths would undergo yet another change in 2011, in the aftermath of the miniseries *Flashpoint*, once again written by Geoff Johns. *Flashpoint* told the story of Barry Allen (who had returned to life during *Final Crisis*) changing the past in order to save his mother's life, but instead accidentally creating a dystopia in the present. With the help of this new world's Batman, Barry restores his world, but outside forces intervene to create a rebooted reality that DC would officially call "The New 52." This reinvention of the DC Universe would see younger, more unsure heroes, bereft of the sense of legacy that was so long a part of DC's imaginary world.

It also rewrote the multiverse, with new versions of Earth-Two and Earth-Three appearing. It was not until the 2015 crossover miniseries *Convergence* that readers would learn how *Flashpoint* affected the full multiverse. *Convergence* reveals that longtime Superman villain Brainiac has evolved powers allowing him to capture cities from throughout the history of the multiverse, in its various incarnations, and transport them to a planet under his control. In the eighth and final issue of the series, Brainiac chooses to divest himself of the multiversal energy he has absorbed by returning each city to its proper time and place. The effort, though, alters and changes the 52 worlds of the multiverse. In two back-to-back double-page spreads by penciller Ethan Van Sciver, we see a variety of Earths, both familiar and new, floating in the cosmic void, the classic visual trope of the multiverse. Behind each Earth are ghostly visions of the denizens of that Earth from the original multiverse, with new versions of the same characters out in front in bold action poses. Brainiac observes this and notes, "Reality is resetting. Stabilizing. Each world has evolved, but they all still exist" (25–26).

The multiverse created in *Infinite Crisis* and *52* had now been subtly changed to reflect the multiverse of both *Final Crisis* and The New 52. This would serve to clear the way for Grant Morrison's sequel to *Final Crisis*, a nine-issue miniseries entitled, fittingly, *The Multiversity*. The series consisted of six one-shot stories set on different worlds in the multiverse, as well as a two-part framing story and a guidebook to the series (and to the multiverse itself). The story, once again, is about the multiverse in crisis, this time from evil multidimensional beings called the Gentry, who live between universes. These creatures are a direct result of the ending of *Final Crisis*, as described in one of the one-shot issues, *The Society of Super-Heroes*: "When the monitor race died, things from outside came to occupy the vacuum they left behind" (17).

Though the story itself revels in all the visual and narrative tropes of the multiverse—worlds overlapping one another, massive destruction and threat on an unthinkable scale, universal vibrations separating different Earths, etc.—it is perhaps the midpoint sourcebook, simply called *The Multiversity Guidebook*, that is most important, in that here Morrison fully fleshes out the entire history and cosmology of the second-phase DC Multiverse. The issue features a complicated "Map of the Multiverse"—designed by artist Rian Hughes—that attempts to categorize the entirety of existence within the imaginary world of DC Comics, as well as a "Multiversity Guidebook" that provides brief biographies of the majority of the 52 Earths (seven Earths are deliberately left as mysteries, to serve as seeds of future stories either from Morrison or other creators).

Narratively, the framing story of the issue also presents, once more, the origin of the multiverse. Not only does Morrison reiterate here the concept established in *Final Crisis* that the entire multiverse exists within an "overmind" that is the blank page, but he also briefly summarizes the entire history of the multiverse up to that point, in typical Morrisonian poetic/elliptical fashion:

> A multitude of coexistent worlds was revealed. A whole spectrum of variations on the theme. A multiverse. Then came the first *Crisis on Infinite Earths*. Where worlds that once had been collapsed were fused together. Where lives were erased—rewritten. And whole realities converged in epic congress. What had been multiverse was universe once more. Unstable, uncertain, post-traumatic. And all the while, forces beyond imagination were at work. . . . And so it was until reality changed again. And changed again. What once had been was rendered unremembered. Re-forgotten. Once more, a multiverse erupted from the fragile unstable universe. New shoots, fresh fractal branches, wormed their way through hypertime and 52 new universes were born. An ordered orrery of worlds. Which were erased and renewed, as continuities rose and fell in waves and troubles. No one knew. No one remembered. Only the Monitors kept a record of it all. . . . When the almighty Monitors died, it went unnoticed. . . . And always behind it all . . . something vast and patient and terrible.
>
> (22–24)

Then, at the very end of this sequence, artist Marcus To portrays the star-filled cosmic hand that has been so central to the multiverse, but this time rather than holding a galaxy it is holding the Orrery of Worlds from *Final Crisis*. The omniscient caption over this panel reads, "What great hand casts the lightning . . . and remakes the world?" (24). After decades of unspoken presumption that the hand originally seen by Kronos in *Green Lantern* #40 was that of the DC Universe's omnipotent God, Morrison poses the question of whose hand it really might have been.

In the series' conclusion ("Superjudge," in *The Multiversity* #2), we presumably learn the answer—an evil entity (and the master of the Gentry) known as "The Empty Hand," who sits upon the blasted remains of a ruined Earth and tells the assembled heroes of the multiverse:

> I have CONCLUDED my assessment of your strength. I have NOTHING to fear from you. The END will come when I decree. Not YET. . . . The Gentry labor to complete the OBLIVION MACHINE. The FINAL CHAPTER of your NEVER-ENDING STORY. . . . My LEGIONS await my command. They feed and grow strong on the starry carcass of our PREVIOUS victim— MULTIVERSE-2! I will CHOOSE when NEXT we meet. BE GONE! EMPTY IS MY HAND!
>
> (44–45)

The Empty Hand then disperses the heroes with a wave of his hand. In this villainous monologue, Morrison clearly hints at a future story yet to be told featuring The Empty Hand, but just as importantly, with this offhanded[4] reference to "Multiverse-2," he indicates that perhaps there is more to the multiverse than just the 52 Earths and surrounding domains we saw in the "Map of the Multiverse." DC Comics' next big multiversal event would prove Morrison correct in this assertion.

Dark Nights: Metal and Phase Three of the DC Multiverse

Following a critically and commercially successful, multi-year run on the main *Batman* title, in 2018 writer Scott Snyder and penciller Greg Capullo were given the chance to tell a story of the larger DC Multiverse, called *Dark Nights: Metal*. Scott Snyder describes the series as, "our own love letter to comic book storytelling at its most joyfully, epically lunatic, and a tribute to the kinds of stories that got me through hard times as a kid, and as an adult. It's about using friendship as a foundation to get through darkness and journey further than you thought you could go" (untitled afterword, 45). In the series, the creative team would indeed focus on heroes fighting their way through ultimate darkness, and winning thanks to a combination of friendship (the legacy of years of stories about the heroes working together) and the crazy multiplicity of storytelling possibilities inherent in an expansive multiverse.

The story of *Dark Nights: Metal* involves the discovery of a realm beyond the multiverse, as described by adventurer, archeologist, and future superhero (as Hawkgirl) Kendra Saunders. In the first issue, she shows the heroes of the Justice League the exact "Map of the Multiverse" from *The Multiversity*, and tells them, "This is a map of what we believe to be our multiverse. Not just our universe, but all the universes made of matter and antimatter in existence. We know of fifty-two. We believe it to be a set number" (21). However, she goes on to explain that she and her team have traced energy emanating from a special type of metal, called Nth Metal, from a place called the Dark Multiverse, which she represents by flipping over the map of the multiverse:

> Everyone believed the building blocks of reality were matter and anti-matter. But not long ago, astronomers discovered a third material. And the scary thing is, it turns out dark matter and dark energy actually make up the great majority of our universe. This stuff we can't see or feel. So now look at the map and imagine Nth Metal connecting us to a realm much older and much vaster than ours, an oceanic, subconscious realm our tiny multiverse floats on.
> (22)

Within that Dark Multiverse, Saunders explains, lives a cosmically powerful being named Barbatos, whom Batman, through his exploration into the science behind the multiverse, has inadvertently set free. The rest of the series shows Barbatos attempting to drag the 52 Earths of the multiverse into the darkness of the Dark Multiverse below, and the Justice League's heroic battle to prevent this.

As the series unfolds, we learn more about the nature of the Dark Multiverse, which one of its darkest creations—a twisted combination of Batman and the Joker known as "The Batman Who Laughs"[5]—describes in the third issue as follows: "See, down in our realm, worlds are created by all you people up here. You fear or hope for something, and it births a world" (9). Later, Superman and Batman learn the history of the Dark Multiverse from Daniel, the Sandman, a cosmic entity who first appeared in the pages of Neil Gaiman's groundbreaking *Sandman* series in the late 1980s and early 1990s.[6] In the fourth issue, Daniel provides yet another slightly updated origin of the multiverse, one that incorporates the Monitor and Anti-Monitor from *Crisis on Infinite Earths*, Morrison's conception of the Orrery of Worlds, as well as Snyder and Capullo's newer ideas:

> From the dark came a great spark of molten potential. The spark created two opposing existences, Matter and Anti-Matter. With them, came the brothers, set to monitor all that had been created, and a third being, tasked to watch over what had yet to come. This being resided at the World Forge, deep in the roiling cauldron of possibility you call the Dark Multiverse. For eons, it hammered out universes from the hopes and fears of all living beings. The most stable worlds rose into the Orrery. For the twisted, unstable worlds, the Forger had a Great Dragon to destroy them and return their energies to the Forge. . . . But the dragon [Barbatos], a being who knew only destruction, killed its master, and thus, worlds that should have been dissolved lived on, and the Forge began to darken. . . . Barbatos desires to pull all worlds into the dark, and he is winning. . . . Any further and Barbatos will be able to bring forth all the nightmares of the Dark Multiverse.
>
> (12–14)

Using a new metal discovered within the seemingly extinguished World Forge, Superman and Batman, along with the rest of the Justice League, restore the Orrery to its proper place, but in doing so inadvertently breach the Source Wall that exists at the boundary of the multiverse.

This action at the climax of *Dark Nights* occurs underneath a series of captions from the journal of Carter Hall, Hawkman, who had previously found himself lost in the Dark Multiverse after attempting to explore and chart it. While Kendra Saunders had believed that there was only darkness and evil lurking below the multiverse, Hall considered himself a detective who wanted to unlock the mysteries within the dark. Earlier in the series, in the second issue, an excerpt from his journal describes the origin of the multiverse as we know it from *Crisis on Infinite Earths*:

> Krona developed a machine to peer into the very core of the universe . . . to see what lay behind it all. And what he saw was a great hand so far back that the very act of looking at it opened up millions of worlds. My point is, the actual origin story of the entire multiverse is about exploration, about discovery . . . [but] it's also a tragedy. . . . See, Krona was reviled for his hubris, for going too far. He became the most hated man in the multiverse. The origin story of our multiverse, it's a cautionary tale. It says explore too far . . . and you may just become the villain of your own story.
>
> (1, 22)

As the Justice League restore the multiverse in the sixth issue, though, we see the now rescued Hall's updated take on this story, one renewed with hope:

> For to be human, at its core, is to question and quest. To seek answers about who we are. Even when—or especially when—these answers are beyond our grasp. And what I have learned is that sometimes that search leads us to the darkest places imaginable. In those times, we need each other to find our way back home. To remember who we are. But after we find our way back to the light, we must remember to reach even higher next time. To look farther. To explore the greatest mysteries and follow the craziest stories . . . because in the end, sometimes it's the most insane, lunatic journeys that push us past what we thought was true . . . and toward what is possible.
>
> (31)

Metatextually, Snyder is making a case here for a return to a wider cosmology beyond a charted map of 52 universes. Instead, the Dark Multiverse—which has the potential for wonder as well as for menace—is a source of possibility, of infinite Earths returned once more to the DC Multiverse. This is underscored by the imagery of the

Source Wall, described as "the very limit of the Multiverse . . . where everything ends" breaking down, with energy coruscating through from "the other side . . . where even greater mysteries lay waiting" (32). That energy takes the form of an open hand, returning to the foundational imagery of the multiverse.

According to Snyder himself, this ending is intended to show that the DC Multiverse has once again expanded beyond the limited 52 Earths of the second phase of the multiverse:

> We thought we knew the entire map of the DC cosmos. We thought we had explored all there was to explore. But now we know that all this time the Multiverse was nothing but a fishbowl, and we've just been dumped into the ocean, unleashing terrifying new threats and wondrous new possibilities.
>
> (quoted in DC All Access 48)

As critic Dave Wittaker notes, in doing this, "DC isn't attempting to refresh its narrative by simple addition or multiplication. Things really feel like some form of cohesion is occurring. An expansion upon and balancing of the equation."

Thus, with the conclusion of *Dark Nights: Metal*, the DC Multiverse moves into a new, third phase, one that is not limited to a singular DC Universe or even a multiverse of 52 Earths. Rather, it is once again a multiverse of infinite possibility, wherein creators, readers, and characters alike will be able to explore the greater possibilities, mysteries, and cosmic threats that lie waiting beyond the now demolished border of what is known. The full, unfettered, expansive multiverse has at last, finally, returned.

Notes

1 In speaking of the repetition of that image (albeit with only two Earths) on the cover of issue #5, Levitz would note, "Few artists save Pérez could illustrate the faces of more than 80 characters and make each one distinct and recognizable. Pérez's composition for issue No. 5 of *Crisis*, 'Worlds in Limbo,' superimposed two merging Earths, which symbolized the coming

changes to DC continuity. . . . The split-face characters that Pérez placed on the midpoint had equivalents on both Earth-One and Earth-Two, a situation that in some cases required death and sacrifice to bring about DC's vision of a unified narrative" (559–584).

2 These Monitors had been introduced in *Countdown to Final Crisis*.

3 Morrison had previously introduced this very metatextual concept in his run on *Animal Man* in the late 1980s, a very heady, experimental book that first made U.S. comics readers take notice of Morrison. For more on *Animal Man*, see Chapter 3.

4 No pun intended.

5 Seemingly a reference to the 1929 film *The Man Who Laughs*, which served as one of the original inspirations for the creation of the character of the Joker.

6 Daniel's appearance is itself an indication of the cosmic level of this series, given that Gaiman—a massively popular writer and pop culture figure with a following well outside of just comic book readers—has a gentleman's agreement with DC Comics that the character will only ever appear with his explicit blessing.

References

Darius, Julian. *Classics on Infinite Earths: The Justice League and DC Crossover Canon*. Edwardsville, IL: Sequart Organization, 2015.

DC All Access. "Justice League: No Justice," *Dark Nights: Metal* 6, May 2018.

Hickey, Andrew. "The Crisis Project: Issue One." *Mindless Ones*. Last modified January 1, 2018. http://mindlessones.com/2018/01/01/the-crisis-project-issue-one/.

Johns, Geoff, Grant Morrison, Greg Rucka, and Mark Waid, writers, Keith Giffen, art breakdowns, et al. "A Year in the Life," *52* 52. Reprinted in *52: Volume Four*, edited by Anton Kawasaki. New York: DC Comics, 2007.

Johns, Geoff, writer, Phil Jimenez, penciller, et al. *Infinite Crisis* 1. Reprinted in *Infinite Crisis*, edited by Anton Kawasaki. New York: DC Comics, 2006.

Johns, Geoff, writer, Phil Jimenez, penciller, et al. *Infinite Crisis* 2. Reprinted in *Infinite Crisis*, edited by Anton Kawasaki. New York: DC Comics, 2006.

Johns, Geoff, writer, Phil Jimenez, penciller, et al. *Infinite Crisis* 7. Reprinted in *Infinite Crisis*, edited by Anton Kawasaki. New York: DC Comics, 2006.

King, Jeff, and Scott Lobdell, writers, Stephen Segovia, Carl Pagulayan, Eduardo Pansica, and Ethan Van Sciver, pencillers, et al. *Convergence* 8. Reprinted in *Convergence*, edited by Jeb Woodward. New York: DC Comics, 2015.

Levitz, Paul. *75 Years of DC Comics: The Art of Modern Mythmaking.* Cologne, Germany: Taschen, 2010.

Morrison, Grant, writer, J.G. Jones, penciller, et al. "D.O.A.: The GOD of WAR," *Final Crisis* 1. Reprinted in *Final Crisis*, edited by Bob Joy. New York: DC Comics, 2009.

Morrison, Grant, writer, Doug Mahnke, penciller, et al. "New Heaven, New Earth," *Final Crisis* 7. Reprinted in *Final Crisis*, edited by Bob Joy. New York: DC Comics, 2009.

Morrison, Grant, writer, Doug Mahnke, penciller, et al. "Superman Beyond," *Final Crisis: Superman Beyond* 1. Reprinted in *Final Crisis*, edited by Bob Joy. New York: DC Comics, 2009.

Morrison, Grant, writer, Doug Mahnke, penciller, et al. "Superman Beyond," *Final Crisis: Superman Beyond* 2. Reprinted in *Final Crisis*, edited by Bob Joy. New York: DC Comics, 2009.

Morrison, Grant, writer, Cameron Stewart, penciller, et al. "Conquerors from the Counter-World," *Multiversity: The Society of Super-Heroes* 1. Reprinted in *The Multiversity*, edited by Jeb Woodward. New York: DC Comics, 2015.

Morrison, Grant, writer, Ivan Reis, penciller, et al. "Superjudge," *The Multiversity* 2. Reprinted in *The Multiversity*, edited by Jeb Woodward. New York: DC Comics, 2015.

Morrison, Grant, writer, Marcus To, penciller, et al. "Maps and Legends," *The Multiversity Guidebook* 1. Reprinted in *The Multiversity*, edited by Jeb Woodward. New York: DC Comics, 2015.

Snyder, Scott, writer, Greg Capullo, penciller, et al. *Dark Nights: Metal* 1. Reprinted in *Dark Nights: Metal—The Deluxe Edition*, edited by Robin Wildman. New York: DC Comics, 2018.

Snyder, Scott, writer, Greg Capullo, penciller, et al. *Dark Nights: Metal* 2. Reprinted in *Dark Nights: Metal—The Deluxe Edition*, edited by Robin Wildman. New York: DC Comics, 2018.

Snyder, Scott, writer, Greg Capullo, penciller, et al. *Dark Nights: Metal* 3. Reprinted in *Dark Nights: Metal—The Deluxe Edition*, edited by Robin Wildman. New York: DC Comics, 2018.

Snyder, Scott, writer, Greg Capullo, penciller, et al. *Dark Nights: Metal* 4. Reprinted in *Dark Nights: Metal—The Deluxe Edition*, edited by Robin Wildman. New York: DC Comics, 2018.

Snyder, Scott, writer, Greg Capullo, penciller, et al. *Dark Nights: Metal* 6. Reprinted in *Dark Nights: Metal—The Deluxe Edition*, edited by Robin Wildman. New York: DC Comics, 2018.

Snyder, Scott. Untitled afterword. *Dark Nights: Metal* 6, May 2018.

Waid, Mark. "Week Fifty-Two Notes." In *52: Volume Four*, edited by Anton Kawasaki. New York: DC Comics, 2007.

Wittaker, Dave. "*Dark Days, Dark Nights* and Taking DC Continuity to the Nth Degree." *Sequart*. Last modified October 5, 2017. http://sequart.org/magazine/67351/dark-days-dark-nights-and-taking-dc-continuity-to-the-nth-degree.

Wolfman, Marv, writer, George Pérez, penciller, et al. "The Summoning!" *Crisis on Infinite Earths* 1. Reprinted in *Crisis on Infinite Earths*, edited by Rick Taylor and Jim Spivey. New York: DC Comics, 2000.

Wolfman, Marv, writer, George Pérez, penciller, et al. "And Thus Shall the World DIE!" *Crisis on Infinite Earths* 4. Reprinted in *Crisis on Infinite Earths*, edited by Rick Taylor and Jim Spivey. New York: DC Comics, 2000.

Wolfman, Marv, writer, George Pérez, penciller, et al. "Worlds in Limbo," *Crisis on Infinite Earths* 5. Reprinted in *Crisis on Infinite Earths*, edited by Rick Taylor and Jim Spivey. New York: DC Comics, 2000.

Wolfman, Marv, writer, George Pérez, penciller, et al. "Beyond the Silent Night," *Crisis on Infinite Earths* 7. Reprinted in *Crisis on Infinite Earths*, edited by Rick Taylor and Jim Spivey. New York: DC Comics, 2000.

Wolfman, Marv, writer, George Pérez, penciller, et al. "Death at the Dawn of Time!" *Crisis on Infinite Earths* 10. Reprinted in *Crisis on Infinite Earths*, edited by Rick Taylor and Jim Spivey. New York: DC Comics, 2000.

Wolfman, Marv, writer, George Pérez, penciller, et al. "Aftershock," *Crisis on Infinite Earths* 11. Reprinted in *Crisis on Infinite Earths*, edited by Rick Taylor and Jim Spivey. New York: DC Comics, 2000.

Wolfman, Marv, writer, George Pérez, penciller, et al. "Final Crisis," *Crisis on Infinite Earths* 12. Reprinted in *Crisis on Infinite Earths*, edited by Rick Taylor and Jim Spivey. New York: DC Comics, 2000.

3 Cartographers of the Multiverse

Unlike many imaginary worlds, there is no prime originator behind the DC Multiverse. In part, this is because the world of DC Comics is itself a conglomeration of individual "worlds"—such as Superman's Metropolis and Batman's Gotham City—created by different people and later put together into one story universe. In addition, the legal owner of the various intellectual properties that make up the DC Multiverse is a business entity, DC Comics (and its corporate owner, Time Warner), rather than a specific individual. While, for example, James Cameron is the primary "subcreator" (to use J.R.R. Tolkien's term) behind the *Avatar* franchise's world of Pandora and George R.R. Martin is the subcreator of Westeros in the *Song of Ice and Fire* series of novels, there is no such individual who is the mastermind of the DC Multiverse. As Grant Morrison puts it in his book *Supergods* (which is half memoir and half his own personalized history of comic books):

> DC's incoherent origins formed an archipelago of island concepts that were slowly bolted together to create a mega-continuity involving multiple parallel worlds that could not only make sense of pre-Silver Age versions of characters like the Flash, but also fit in new acquisitions from defunct companies that made Marvel's universe look provincial.
>
> (114)

The DC Multiverse, then, is not the handiwork of just one or two creators. Rather, during the long history of DC Comics, several writers have come to the fore as explorers of the multiverse, as it were, expanding upon the various worlds and ideas created by others while developing original concepts of their own to continue to add to that tapestry. Though these are certainly "subcreators" of the DC Multiverse, in Tolkien's sense, they are also equally *cartographers* of that multiverse, teasing out and refining previously existing concepts as well as charting new courses for future narrative potential. This chapter will explore how four specific writers mentioned in the previous two chapters—Gardner Fox, Marv Wolfman, Geoff Johns, and Grant Morrison—worked to define the contours of the DC Multiverse, thereby showcasing how that multiverse could be used as a central tenet of storytelling in the imaginary world(s) of DC Comics.

Gardner Fox

Writer Gardner Fox was one half of a team—along with editor Julie Schwartz—who introduced the concept of the multiverse to readers of DC Comics. Whereas Schwartz was the guiding force behind reviving the heroes of the Justice Society in sleeker, modern versions, thereby kicking off the "Silver Age" of superhero comics, it was Fox who developed the idea of the multiverse in order to create an in-story link between the two eras of heroes. He defined the parameters of the multiverse and justified the logic of its existence, a pseudoscientific explanation of worlds vibrating at difference frequencies that is still part of the multiversal mythos through to the present.

It is perhaps fitting that Fox was the creator who linked the heroes of two distinct eras in the history of DC Comics, because he was one of the few creators who consistently worked in comics throughout both periods. According to comics historian Bill Schelly, Fox:

> was one of the main creators when comic books were born in the late 1930s to begin comics' Golden Age and provided some of the best stories when DC's superheroes were recreated in the early 1960s for the Silver Age. . . . Fox estimated he wrote more than 4,000 comic book stories during the course of his career, and well over 50 million words in all.

(195)

In part, Schelly notes, this is because Fox didn't just write superhero stories, but was able to transition into science fiction, westerns, and romance comics in the period during which superhero comics were out of favor.

In their comprehensive history of comic books from the 1950s through the 1990s, *The Comic Book Heroes*, Gerard Jones and Will Jacobs explain that Fox's contribution to superhero comics began well before the development of the multiverse, when he was a crucial figure behind the groundbreaking idea that various heroes from the same publisher all lived in the same world:

> When Fox was young and inspired he gave comics a whole con-
> stellation of characters for nothing but page rates: the original
> Flash, Hawkman, Sandman, Dr. Fate, and Starman. . . . Through
> the 1940s he poured out story after story about his colorful crime-
> fighters, but the best of them were his fifty-eight pagers about
> the heroes' combined adventures in *All-Star Comics*, starring the
> Justice Society of America. Fox invented the idea of a hero team,
> and although the JSA was often copied during the 1940s, it was
> never equaled. When Schwartz picked him to write the new Justice
> League, he affirmed the continuity of superhero comics.
>
> (35)

Fox was, in many ways, the living link between the two eras of super-hero comics, which would soon become, thanks to him and Schwartz, two distinct parallel Earths.

In creating the concept of Earth-Two as a home to the older super-heroes,[1] Fox was able to cater to longtime fans (including himself) who were fond of those older characters while still maintaining focus on the forward-looking heroes he and other creators had developed for Schwartz. Schelly calls this "perhaps one of the scripter's greatest contributions to comic fandom," as well as "a huge creative shot-in-the-arm for the comic book industry as a whole" (196). Furthermore:

> Through the parallel Earth theory, Fox gave fans what they had
> been clamoring for all along—a chance to see some of the great
> Golden Age heroes in the current issues of their favorite Silver

Age comic books. It also gave comics publishers a hook to not only use older popular characters, but also to create new ones on what has become a bevy of parallel worlds in their various universes.

(35)

One of the earliest voices in fandom, Roy Thomas (who would not too long after become the first fan to transition into a professional comic book writer and editor), backs up this "clamor," noting that he and his friend Jerry Bails, who together produced the first comics fanzine, *Alter Ego*, "were among the most vocal and persistent" of voices wanting to see a return of the Justice Society, "but ours were hardly the lone voices calling out in the four-color wilderness. These mostly adult readers carried the bring-back-the-JSA banner both in comics fanzines and in letters to editors" (16).

From the outset, then, the DC Multiverse was being used to serve multiple masters by appealing to both a sense of legacy that was pleasing to fans and the playful possibilities of multiplicity that appealed to editors and publishers eager to expand the storytelling possibilities (and thus inherently the profit possibilities) of the DC Comics line as a whole. Fox would continue to explore these twin through lines in the six JLA/JSA team-ups he would write during his tenure as scripter on *Justice League of America*. Through each of these crossover stories, he would feature a rotating group of JSA member so as to give exposure to the various "Golden Age" heroes he couldn't fit into one story, while at the same time he would forge ahead with creating new concepts, such as the Crime Syndicate's Earth-Three, the cosmically threatening Anti-Matter Man, and the android Red Tornado.

The Gardner Fox story that perhaps most cogently expresses the potential he saw in the multiverse came in 1967's *Justice League of America* #55 and #56, titled "The Super-Crisis That Struck Earth-Two!" and "The Negative-Crisis on Earths One-Two!" The primary plot of this story involves an alien energy that transforms average people into supervillains, as well as turning four members of the two teams against their fellow heroes. What's most important about this story, though, is that it showcases just how far Fox was willing to diverge

Earth-One from Earth-Two. Whereas previous stories guest-starring the Justice Society had simply shown the heroes as they were when they were originally published, albeit having aged a few decades, in this story Fox took Batman's sidekick, Robin, in a direction radically different from his core conceptualization.

Unlike some of the JSA members, such as the Flash or Green Lantern, Robin didn't just have the same superhero name and powers as an Earth-One hero, but also the same secret identity and backstory. This was a characteristic shared by Superman, Batman, and Wonder Woman as well, since all four characters had been continually published from the 1940s through to the 1960s, and thus there was never any need to "revive" their core concept as Schwartz had done with the Flash and other heroes. Now, though, Fox made a decision to take advantage of the Earth-Two concept in order to differentiate between the teenage sidekick version of Robin from Earth-One and the Robin of Earth-Two who was now grown to adulthood. This version of Robin is no longer just Batman's sidekick, or even his partner, but rather his own hero, wearing a costume created by penciller Mike Sekowsky that combines his classic yellow cape with Batman's gray bodysuit to indicate how he has stepped up to assume his mentor's mantle.[2]

Indeed, it is implied that the only reason Robin hasn't taken on the name Batman is because Bruce Wayne hasn't yet retired. As Robin explains to the JSA in issue #55 after being announced as their new member:

> I want to convey Batman's best wishes! Though he's in semi-retirement, he still goes out on special cases—which is what's keeping him from attending this meeting! . . . I want to thank the Justice Society for fulfilling my life's ambition to be a member of such a distinguished group! I'll do my best to prove worthy of the honor!

(13)

Thus, Fox is able to make real change to a character on Earth-Two that would not have been allowed for the "primary" hero on Earth-One.

The following year's team-up, in *Justice League of America* #64 and #65, would prove to be Fox's final story for the title, and his final scripts featuring his own co-creations, the Justice Society and the Justice League (which might explain why issue #64 featured only the JSA, without the JLA even making an appearance). Sadly, his career would go on to end with a whimper, without the fanfare one would think such a foundational figure might deserve. By 1971, he had been cut loose by DC and Julius Schwarz, forced to scrounge for work. A short stint that year writing *Red Wolf*—a title about a Native American hero— for Marvel would, according to Jones and Jacobs, "prove to be Fox's last series, the quiet departure of a seminal comic book writer who still seemed to have something to offer, but nothing that fandom was looking for" (166).

Marv Wolfman

One of Gardner Fox's biggest fans, Roy Thomas was the first person to make the transition from writing for fanzines about comic books to actually writing comic books *for* the major publishers. He was hardly the last to do so, however, and several generations of fans-turned-writers would come to dominate the industry in his wake. These writers tended to be a different breed than the professional science-fiction/pulp writers, such as Fox, who had previously helmed most superhero titles. Rather than just seeing comic book writing as a job to pay the bills, they viewed it as more of a calling, and an opportunity to do something creative with the characters they had grown up loving.

One such individual was writer Marv Wolfman, who, like Thomas, began his career as a fanzine publisher. Among other publications, his fanzine *Stories of Suspense* would publish early work by many creators who would go on to professional success, including the first published story by none other than Stephen King.[3] Bill Schelly explains how Wolfman began his professional career thanks in part to leveraging the relationship he had built with a few DC editors:

Due to his talent, persistence and proximity, Wolfman became one of the first fans to penetrate the "closed shop" barrier that DC Comics presented to fandom at the time. . . . His breakthrough took place in 1967, with a script he wrote on spec for *Blackhawk*, one of his favorite comics that had fallen on hard times. Although he mailed it to the editor at the time, that editor never got back to him. Marv thought the story had been lost, but a year later Dick Giordano took over the editor's job, found the script (in its unopened envelope), and bought the story. Simultaneously, Joe Orlando had Marv re-dialog a script that another writer had written. Wolfman had scripts published in both Dick Giordano's and Joe Orlando's mystery-oriented comic books.

(188)

Before too long, Wolfman would move from mystery and horror-themed stories (both at DC and, later, Marvel) to crafting superhero stories, including the extremely popular series *The New Teen Titans* that he co-created with penciller George Pérez. At the same time, he was also working as an editor, first as Marvel's editor-in-chief and later as a senior editor at DC. It was in the latter role that he first started conceiving his greatest contribution to the DC Multiverse—its destruction—in the pages *Crisis on Infinite Earths*.

According to "Crisis Mail: Crisis Beginnings," a text piece he wrote on the inside covers of the first issue of *Crisis*, Wolfman first began thinking about the DC Multiverse when a fan letter published in 1981's *Green Lantern* #143 asked about a continuity mix-up. This led Wolfman to consider how complicated the DC Comics imaginary world might seem to readers:

> Characters crossed earths because writers or editors couldn't keep straight who lived where and when. Why did some characters age and others stay young? . . . [T]he problems continued. We had two sets of Supermans, Batmans, Flashes, Wonder Womans, Green Lanterns, etc. etc. We also had a dozen different Earths. And so on and so on and so on. Writers like to complicate matters and what began as a dream of a story—"Flash of Two Worlds"—had turned into a nightmare. DC continuity was so confusing no new reader could easily understand it while older readers had to keep miles-long lists to set things straight. And the writers . . . well, we were always stumbling over each other trying to figure out simple answers to difficult questions.

Thus, Wolfman—along with editor Len Wein, penciller George Pérez (both of whom co-plotted some of the series), researcher Peter Sanderson, fellow writer/editor Roy Thomas, and DC executives Dick Giordano and Jennette Kahn—dreamed up *Crisis on Infinite Earths*. As he explained in the same text piece:

> For the past several years many people have suggested 'fixing up' the DC Universe. Simplifying it. . . . Well, CRISIS ON INFINITE EARTHS will attempt such a repair job. By series end DC will have a consistent and more easily understandable universe to play with.

As discussed in the previous chapter, by the end of *Crisis*, the DC Multiverse had become the DC Universe, with one singular reality and no multiple Earths. Whether or not what resulted was a simplified, consistent, more easily understandable universe is entirely debatable, given the multiple continuity confusions that arose as a direct result of *Crisis*, but it's clear that Wolfman's goal from the outset was to bring new readers to DC with an epic tale that would create one story universe going forward, a singular imaginary world rather than a multiverse of many imaginary worlds. He opened the letters page (called "Crisis Mail") of the third issue by writing, "Welcome to the third issue of CRISIS ON INFINITE EARTHS, DC Comics' 12-part maxi-series that will, by the time we're done, streamline the entire DC multiverse into one coherent universe with a consistent past, present, and future" (26). In the fourth issue's letters page, he wrote:

> There's nothing wrong with doing a comic intended to sell toys— DC did SUPER POWERS last year. However, the CRISIS was created solely to make the DC Universe more accessible to the largest number of readers, which means our concerns are toward story, plot, and characterization.
>
> (27)

Nor has Wolfman's belief that the multiverse needed to die lessened over time, even as the multiverse made its resurgence. In his introduction to the *Crisis* collected edition, he would note:

> CRISIS brought readers to DC Comics, and that was, of course, its purpose. . . . The idea was to simplify the universe, and we did that. After a few rough starts, I would like to think those who followed us understand the need to keep working to broaden the reader base, not to shrink it by sticking with outdated continuity.
>
> (6–7)

As recently as 2018, in an introduction to a companion volume to *Crisis*, Wolfman reiterated this satisfaction with what the series achieved:

> In 1985—Earth Standard Time—George Pérez and I . . . deliberately, and without provocation or regret, murdered in cold blood an infinite number of worlds and universes. When we were done, only one universe remained. The infinite became the singular. And those who lived on that solitary Earth cheered.
>
> (5)

In order to make this newly singular universe work, Wolfman fought to have none of the characters recall the events of *Crisis*, so that even the memories of the multiverse were exorcised from DC Comics. Though the question of who actually remembered what became muddled over time, at the end of *Crisis* the heroes still remembered the events of the series, something Wolfman disliked. He noted in an interview at the time that:

> My feeling was that, if anyone remembered, there'd be somebody discussing it, and, once you discuss it, you have to refer to it, and once you refer to it, you keep bringing up the specter of Multiple Earths. It bothered me greatly. To me, that was the worst part of the whole book, the fact that I had to compromise on that issue. However, the editorial staff at the time felt that the heroes, at least, should remember Crisis.
>
> (quoted in Waid 55)

For Wolfman, then, the multiverse was more a hindrance than it was an engine of storytelling potential, and he wanted it gone for good.

He deliberately worked to eliminate multiplicity within the DC Universe while creating a sense of legacy that all took place in one reality, as was the case at Marvel Comics.

In another interview at the time of *Crisis*'s publication, he bluntly stated that part of his goal was to eliminate the goofier aspects of DC's past, many of which were tied to the multiverse:

> What we're trying to do: If it's not restated, it did not happen. The beauty of the way we're ending the Crisis, and the way we're rebuilding everything, is that all of that's gone. All the dumb stuff is gone, and somebody's really going to have to go out of his way to bring it back. . . . It's corrective history. There's a big eraser that's gone over all of it. If an editor deems a character or storyline worthy enough to bring back, okay—but I don't think we should be held responsible for past mistakes.
>
> (quoted in O'Neill 25)

With *Crisis*, then, Wolfman didn't so much chart the multiverse as he did provide one last, gorgeous map of it that he immediately tore to shreds. In the aftermath, a new, simpler map—the "New Earth" of the DC Universe—was created. Thus, the DC Multiverse went from its expansive first phase to its contained second phase, beginning with two decades of dormancy.

Ironically, though, the entire exercise of Wolfman's complex maneuvering in *Crisis* and its aftermath was perhaps unnecessary. Though he, and others on the DC staff, may have felt the multiverse was "dumb" or confusing, readers didn't necessarily agree. Grant Morrison, for example, claims in *Supergods* that:

> There were complaints that the parallel-worlds system was too unwieldy and hard to understand, when in fact it was systematic, logical, and incredibly easy to navigate, particularly for young minds that were made for this kind of careful categorization of facts and figures.
>
> (214)

Similarly, Gerard Jones and Will Jacobs note that "there wasn't much evidence that anyone was bothered by the confusion" of the multiverse, and indeed:

> Readers always seemed to have fun learning to keep the two Earths straight . . . but DC people were in the habit of asking themselves what Marvel was doing better. Some feared the complexity of the DC "multiverse" was an obstacle to young readers climbing aboard.
>
> (294)

More evocatively, they claim that "*Crisis* was to be the death, not just of Earth-2, Earth-3, and all the rest of them, but of the DC that was" (295). They were not the only readers who felt like this. Many fans truly loved the multiverse, and the way it embodied and honored both the historical legacy and creative multiple variety of DC Comics. They were sad to see it go and longed for its return.

Geoff Johns

Much like Marv Wolfman, Geoff Johns was a fan of DC Comics long before he ever became a writer for the company. After graduating from college with a film degree, he worked as an assistant to Richard Donner (who had directed the first two *Superman* films) before breaking into comics in 1999 with a series he co-created called *Stars and S.T.R.I.P.E.* Though the main character of this series, Courtney Whitmore, was a new creation, she was also a legacy character, inheriting the suit, powers, and code name of "Golden Age" hero the Star-Spangled Kid. In fact, she was the stepdaughter of the original Star-Spangled Kid's sidekick, Stripesy, who followed Courtney around in a specially designed suit of armor to help keep her out of trouble.

The seeds of Johns' future work for DC were established in his short run on *Stars and S.T.R.I.P.E.* Though the series only lasted for 12 issues, it featured a panoply of guest stars from across the DC Universe, focused on the intergenerational nature of the DC heroes, and reinvigorated lost or forgotten characters and concepts from throughout DC's long history. He would later go on to much longer runs on two titles intimately associated with the history of the then-dormant multiverse— *The Flash* and *JSA*. In both titles, without making overt references to the lost multiverse, Johns focused overwhelmingly on one of its key ideas: legacy.

In *The Flash*, the titular hero was now Wally West, Barry Allen's sidekick who had assumed the mantle following Barry's death in *Crisis*. Wally was forever aware of whose shoes he was trying to fill, and Johns even found some time-traveling narrative tricks to bring Barry in for a few guest appearances. Similarly, Johns' work on *JSA* (along with, at times, co-writers James Robinson and David Goyer) emphasized the idea that the Justice Society were the elder statesman of superheroes. The title was even more focused on the concept of legacy than *The Flash* was, with the older heroes (most of whom had found magical ways to stay young, since on the post-*Crisis* New Earth the Justice Society's early adventures all took place around World War II) serving as mentors to newer, younger characters.

Johns' work on these two titles—along with the miniseries *Green Lantern: Rebirth*, which brought back to life classic Green Lantern Hal Jordan by justifying and reinterpreting a decade's worth of complex continuity—led DC's editorial and executive team to tap him for the sequel to *Crisis on Infinite Earths*. It was in *Infinite Crisis* that Johns first showed his affection for the multiverse, continuing to take a look at the legacy of heroes in DC's imaginary world while at the same time utilizing multiplicity in order to make a larger narrative point about those heroes.

In its celebration of the various colors and characters of the DC Universe, *Infinite Crisis* certainly hits some operatic heights of epic storytelling. Grant Morrison would later describe it in *Supergods* as:

> dense and arcane, a combination of guidebook and comic book that both thrilled and comforted DC's core audience. Geoff Johns' work was always perfectly tuned to the exact sensibilities of the DC fan-boy demographic, and he knew when to roll out characterizations they were familiar with and when to add shock or

novelty. But it was hard to imagine this concordance appealing to a wider audience. Its raisons d'être were specialist concerns, lacking mainstream appeal, although as an introduction to the expansive, bewildering DC virtual reality it was hard to beat.

(387–388)

For Johns, though, the key beats of *Infinite Crisis* were clearly about character, rather than large-scale scope. He used the return of the multiverse to talk about the heroes at the core of the action, rather than for the sake of the action itself, and to comment on metanarrative aspects of how those characters had been presented over DC's history.

As explained in Chapter 2, the narrative of *Infinite Crisis* revolves around the last survivors of the DC Multiverse returning to New Earth in order to "correct" what had happened at the end of *Crisis*. From their perspective, having departed the universe during a time just before comics narratives began to turn darker and more mature, the DC Universe of the prior 20 years had gone seriously wrong, and needed to be fixed. Through a monologue in *Infinite Crisis* #1 from the Superman of Earth-Two, presented in captions overlaying events from those 20 years, such as Superman's death, the vicious Bane breaking Batman's back, and Hal Jordan turning villainous, Johns provides meta-commentary on the darkness of the DC Universe since *Crisis*:

From our place, we watched this new Earth grow. The potential was there. And it started off so well. So full of hope. I felt confident Earth was in good hands. But soon after, we learned there was something inherently wrong. This new Earth was anything but better. A darkness seemed to spread. Warping the heroes' lives. Some died. Others lost their way. We watched for years, hoping everyone would find inspiration again. But as we continued to look on . . . things got worse.

(59–60)

In the second issue, he explains to his cousin, Power Girl, that he intends to rectify this situation by bringing back Earth-Two:

This Earth you've been on since I left . . . it's corrupted, Kara.
How do they live like this? . . . Joyless. Alexander has kept
records, he's shown me so many things the people you work with
have done. To their adversaries. And to each other. They alter
minds. They kill. I never understood why I survived when others
didn't. Or what my true purpose in this universe was. Not until
now. When the universe was reborn, Earth-One became the primary world. The scraps of the remaining worlds were folded into
it. But I finally realize—we saved the wrong Earth. . . . This corrupted and darkened Earth must be forgotten as ours was . . . so
that the right Earth can return.

(71–72)

Superman's final speech on the subject comes when Alexander
Luthor (through villainous means of which Superman is unaware)
actually does recreate Earth-Two, which Superman thinks will save
the life of his aging wife, Lois. Despite the planet's return, though,
Lois dies, and Superman becomes enraged, lashing out against New
Earth's Superman. During a pause in their battle in the fifth issue, the
Superman of Earth-Two rants:

[Y]ou, Superman, could've stopped this before it started. You
should have! You should have led them to a better tomorrow.
Instead, when the universe needed its greatest heroes, they refused
to stand together. You had the opportunity to make that Earth
into the perfect world it had the potential to be and you wasted it!
That's why I had to come here. That's why my Lois died!

(160)

In response, the Superman of New Earth simply says, "If you're
from this Earth it can't be perfect. Because a perfect Earth doesn't
need a Superman" (160). This reaction brings the Earth-Two
Superman to his senses, and he realizes that he's been misled by
Alexander Luthor into searching for a kind of nostalgic perfection
that never actually existed.

Through this series of melodramatic speeches, Johns is able to use the interaction of the two Supermen in order to make a larger point. The Earth-Two Superman represented the complaints of fans who felt that superhero stories had gotten too dark and violent, and who pined for the simpler, more wholesome stories of yesteryear. The reaction from New Earth's Superman, though, reiterates Johns' key point in *Infinite Crisis*—that superhero stories are inherently about overcoming great odds, and that as a narrative medium they can only exist as a reaction to an imperfect world.

Johns' affection for the multiverse would carry over from *Infinite Crisis* to the ending of *52*, where, built on the events of *Infinite Crisis*, the multiverse returned. He would utilize that reborn multiverse in several future titles he worked on, exploring the reborn Earth-Two in *Justice Society of America* as well as bringing the previously out-of-continuity apocalyptic story *Kingdom Come* into the reborn multiverse as Earth-22. He would also bring back Earth-Prime's now evil Superboy, and even *Crisis*'s big villain the Anti-Monitor, in various series on which he worked. For Johns, the multiverse continued to present an opportunity to use multiplicity in order to directly explore legacy, by holding various iterations of heroes up to one another so as to comment on, for example, the deeper mythology of what it means to be Superman. As an obsessive devotee of continuity, his focus is primarily on how the multiverse impacts upon the characters of DC's main line and what it means for those characters going forward. Other creators, though, seem more interested in the epic backdrop that the multiverse can provide for massive, apocalyptic narratives.

Grant Morrison

Grant Morrison actually began exploring the DC Multiverse years before Geoff Johns ever broke into comics. A Scottish writer, he first made a name writing for British weekly comics such as *2000 AD*, for which he created *Zenith*, a deconstruction of superheroes and celebrity culture that featured Morrison's own take on a multiverse.

As Morrison explains it in *Supergods*, over four volumes of *Zenith* he and artist/co-creator Steve Yeowell:

> chronicled our hero's reluctant entry into a massive parallel-worlds story that led inexorably to the origin of everything and one of those apocalyptic final battles so beloved of comic-book creators. In our version, instead of banding together to save the multiverse, the superheroes of the various parallel worlds spent twenty-six installments arguing and losing the plot.
>
> (213)

His next foray into exploring the multiverse took place in a much more traditional superhero milieu—that of DC Comics. In a 26-issue run on the series *Animal Man*, Morrison took a C-level character and turned him into a working-class family man who gradually became aware of the fact that he was only a character in a comic book. This story is what first brought Morrison to the attention of American readers, and would pave the way for the heady, experimental, metatextual narratives that he would bring to all of his superhero writing for DC.

Along the path to the title character's self-revelation, *Animal Man* would actually bring back the multiverse, albeit very temporarily. In issue #23, in a story not coincidentally entitled "Crisis," the Psycho-Pirate—a lesser-known villain who was the only character to truly remember the multiverse after the events of *Crisis*—gains the ability to bring back ghosts of the multiverse, beginning with several members of Earth-Three's Crime Syndicate. He tells these returned characters, "You *didn't* die. Nothing really dies. You were right here. In my head all the time. I'm the only one who remembered the way it was before. And now you're back. You're all coming back" (135). Later in the same issue, he happily exclaims, "This is fantastic! More! More! You're all so wonderful. Why did they ever have to remove you from continuity? You'd have made for marvelous stories" (144). However, as more and more worlds and characters emerge from his mind, the Psycho-Pirate finds himself unable to prevent himself from thinking darker thoughts:

> It's neverending. All these worlds. Oh, there's a world here I don't
> want to think about, but I can't seem to help it. It's coming up to
> the surface like a bug hungry fish. A bad world. A world where
> everything's gone wrong. Who makes these awful worlds? Whose
> ideas was this?
>
> (149)

From this dark world arises a violent, insane, evil version of Superman,
whom Animal Man defeats in the following issue, "Purification Day."
Overwhelmed by the energies he's unleashed, the Psycho-Pirate begins
to fade away, but as he does so he tells Animal Man:

> It's not so bad to be taken out of the continuity. It was nice, wasn't
> it? Nice to see all those old characters for one last time. Just the
> way I'd remembered them. I wish they'd stayed. They make the
> world more interesting.
>
> (174)

In his earliest work for the publisher, Morrison metatextually declared
his love of the DC Multiverse, and the worlds full of characters it contained. He would further exhibit this affection during his run on the
series *JLA*. 2000's *JLA: Earth 2*, an original graphic novel co-created
with artist (and frequent Morrison collaborator) Frank Quitely, was
the pair's version of Gardner Fox and Mike Sekowsky's introduction of the Crime Syndicate in the 1964 JLA/SA team-up, "Crisis on
Earth-Three!" For the graphic novel, Morrison eschewed the appearance of the JSA, and instead explored what it would be like for the
Justice League to meet their opposite number from a parallel universe.
Morrison expanded on a small piece of Fox's original story—that on
Earth-One the heroes always win, while on Earth-Three the villains
always win—to produce meta-commentary about the cyclical nature
of superhero stories, while at the same time clearly reveling in showcasing the depravity of the League's evil doubles. However, because
it was created post-*Crisis* but pre-*Infinite Crisis*, *JLA: Earth 2* never
actually mentions the multiverse, instead vaguely alluding to the idea
of parallel universes without any expansion on the concept. Even when

it was off limits, Morrison still found a way to showcase some of his favored concepts of the then-dormant multiverse.

It's perhaps no surprise, then, that Morrison espoused admiration in *Supergods* for the multiverse and its storytelling potential:

> By spreading a given brand across multiple versions of a character designed to appeal to different sections of his audience, Julie [Schwartz] had invented a trick that would be adopted as the industry standard. . . . The idea of infinite worlds, each with its own history and its own superheroes, was intoxicating and gave DC an even more expansive canvas.
>
> (111)

He would also explain rather clearly that it is the inherent multiplicity of the multiverse that he finds so engaging:

> I think it's just a primal thing, seeing the variants of characters—seeing the versions of things. What would Superman be like if he were a vampire, or Batman be like if he were a werewolf. We're so familiar with these archetypes and these characters that just giving them a little twist seems to be one of the basic thrills of comic books. The whole idea of the "road not taken." We've often thought of alternative versions of our own lives, so I think people like to read about these characters having alternative lives and taking different paths and making different choices.
>
> (quoted in Martin)

It wouldn't be until several decades after the conclusion of *Animal Man* that Morrison was able to fully explore the multiverse, in 2008's *Final Crisis* and 2014's *The Multiversity* (both of which were discussed in greater depth in Chapter 2). Morrison's deliberate goal with *The Multiversity*, though, was not merely to enjoy creating a story featuring the DC Multiverse, but also to open the way for future creators to further explore the worlds he had charted. In his original proposal for the series, he notes:

Each issue takes place on a different parallel world from the DC Multiverse and functions as a number one issue and bible for potential series which could be spun off in a line of Multiverse books. Each issue is drawn by a different artist. The books can be read independently but together they tell an epic tale of cosmic villainy and heroism. The series redefines the Multiverse, separating it off from the DCU proper so that it can be developed as its own rich playground before we eventually do the big crossover event where our heroes meet their counterparts for the first time. . . . This is our chance to see a wider spread of worlds and check in with some of the more interesting of the 52 universes.

(93)

Whereas Marv Wolfman and Geoff Johns cared more about character and consistency than they did the potential narrative expansiveness of the multiverse, Morrison seems to be more in the vein of Gardner Fox, with a desire to use the DC Multiverse to revive and renew older ideas while still leaving room for new ones. It is noteworthy, to that end, that the worlds Morrison explores in *The Multiversity* are a mix of updated Earths from the old multiverse, such as Earth-Prime and Earth-5 (home of Captain Marvel), alongside new creations, such as Earth-16, featuring the bored celebrity children of the Justice League.

He also, to a degree, succeeded in his goal of paving the way for future stories of the multiverse: in late 2018, DC launched a new series called *Freedom Fighters* set on Earth-10 (the updated, Nazi-dominated Earth-X), and picking up where Morrison last left that Earth in *The Multiversity*. According to the writer of the series, Rob Venditti, telling the story of a world in the DC Multiverse that isn't the "main" universe of Earth-Zero is freeing in the way that Morrison had intended:

It's a lot of fun because you get to just kind of build everything from scratch and really get to throw a lot of concepts out there and it's something that takes place in the wider DC multiverse but not being set on this Earth means it isn't as constrained as other stories might be. We're really drawing from the *Multiversity* one shot, so that's established some elements but we're really working a lot from scratch.

(quoted in Downey)

In many ways, then, Morrison is the most straightforward cartographer of the DC Multiverse, creating a panoply of ideas for other creators to explore further, even going so far as to create a literal map of the multiverse as a part of the guidebook to *The Multiversity*.

Even more recently, Morrison has explained that as he interprets the cosmology of DC Comics, the DC Multiverse explored in *The Multiversity* is just one of many (an idea that seems to have become part of DC canon with the conclusion to *Dark Knights: Metal*, as discussed in Chapter 2). According to the writer, there isn't just one or two multiverses, but rather "as many as we need. . . . There's, like, little champagne bubbles in a glass" (quoted in Rogers). This panoply of multiverses gives him, as well as other creators, the potential to tell stories that are part of the larger DC Comics imaginary world but don't necessarily fit within the realm of the charted multiverse: "I've got a bunch of stories that don't quite fit into continuity that I've always wanted to tell, and this was an opportunity to do those things and find a home for them" (quoted in Rogers).

Perhaps in the nascent third phase of the DC Multiverse, there will be a return to the anything-goes spirit of Julius Schwartz and Gardner Fox, as embodied by Grant Morrison, Scott Snyder, Robert Venditti, and others, where the multiverse can be a useful tool for telling powerful, moving stories. The twin pillars of legacy and multiplicity that are so inherent to the DC Multiverse lend themselves to a wide variety of narrative potential as part of the future world-building of DC Comics. Indeed, this is why the idea of an expansive multiverse, as refined by the creators at DC over the past half a century, has become key to several adaptations of the comics into other media, as well as serving as inspiration to other comic book companies, as we will see in the next chapter.

Notes

1 Jones and Jacobs attribute the idea of using a parallel universe to bring back Jay Garrick in "Flash of Two Worlds!" to Schwartz (as does Schwartz himself, in various interviews), while Fox believes it was his concept. Either way, it was ultimately Fox who was credited as sole writer for the issue, indicating that he, at the very least, refined that idea into the form that eventually saw publication. As Fox himself would note in an interview,

"It probably evolved out of one of those plot conferences when we batted ideas back and forth. I'm not sure, and I don't think Julie is, either" (quoted in Thomas 18).

2　Though this may have also been an attempt to capitalize on the craze around the then-popular *Batman* live-action TV series.

3　This was, however, a reprinting of that story, which had previously appeared in a lesser-known fanzine (see Schelly 186–187).

References

Downey, Meg. "DC's Freedom Fighters Make Their Triumphant, Nazi-Punching Return." *Comic Book Resources*. Last modified September 13, 2018. www.cbr.com/dc-freedom-fighters-nazi-punching-new-series/.

Fox, Gardner, writer, Mike Sekowsky, penciller, and Julius Schwartz, editor, et al. "The Super-Crisis That Struck Earth-Two!" *Justice League of America* 55. Reprinted in *Crisis on Multiple Earths Volume 2*, edited by Nick J. Napolitano. New York: DC Comics, 2002.

Johns, Geoff, writer, Phil Jimenez, penciller, et al. *Infinite Crisis* 1. Reprinted in *Infinite Crisis*, edited by Anton Kawasaki. New York: DC Comics, 2006.

Johns, Geoff, writer, Phil Jimenez, penciller, et al. *Infinite Crisis* 2. Reprinted in *Infinite Crisis*, edited by Anton Kawasaki. New York: DC Comics, 2006.

Johns, Geoff, writer, Phil Jimenez, penciller, et al. *Infinite Crisis* 5. Reprinted in *Infinite Crisis*, edited by Anton Kawasaki. New York: DC Comics, 2006.

Jones, Gerard and Will Jacobs. *The Comic Book Heroes: The First History of Modern Comic Books from the Silver Age to the Present*. Rocklin, CA: Prima Publishing, 1997.

Martin, Garrett. "Grant Morrison Merges String Theory with Superheroes in DC's *Multiversity*." *Paste*. Last modified August 20, 2014. www.pastemagazine.com/articles/2014/08/across-the-universes-grant-morrison-merges-string.html.

Morrison, Grant. "Original proposal for THE MULTIVERSITY." In *The Multiversity 1 & 2 Director's Cut*. New York: DC Comics, 2016.

Morrison, Grant. *Supergods: What Masked Vigilantes, Miraculous Mutants, and a Sun God from Smallville Can Teach Us About Being Human*. New York: Spiegel & Grau, 2011.

Morrison, Grant, writer, Chas Truog, penciller et al. "Crisis," *Animal Man* 23. Reprinted in *Animal Man: Deus Ex Machina*, edited by Scott Nybakken. New York: DC Comics, 2003.

Morrison, Grant, writer, Chas Truog, penciller et al. "Purification Day," *Animal Man* 24. Reprinted in *Animal Man: Deus Ex Machina*, edited by Scott Nybakken. New York: DC Comics, 2003.

O'Neill, Pat. "Spotlight: Crisis on Infinite Earths," *David Anthony Kraft's Comics Interview* 26, 1985.

Rogers, Vaneta. "MORRISON Divulges 'Weird' Stories for BATMAN: BLACK & WHITE and MULTIVERSITY TOO." *Newsarama*. Last modified July 15, 2015. www.newsarama.com/25243-morrison-reveals-weird-stories-for-batman-black-white-and-multiversity-too.html.

Schelly, Bill. *Founders of Comic Fandom: Profiles of 90 Publishers, Dealers, Collectors, Writers, Artists and Other Luminaries of the 1950s and 1960s.* Jefferson, NC: McFarland & Company, 2010.

Thomas, Roy. "Crises on Finite Earths: The Justice League-Society Team-Ups (1963–1985)," *Alter Ego*, Winter 2001.

Waid, Mark. "Making a Crisis of It: The Creators Reflect . . ." *Amazing Heroes* 91. March 1986.

Wolfman, Marv. "Crisis Mail: Crisis Beginnings," *Crisis on Infinite Earths* 1. April 1985.

Wolfman, Marv. "Crisis Mail: Cooperation, DC Style," *Crisis on Infinite Earths* 3. June 1985.

Wolfman, Marv. "Crisis Mail," *Crisis on Infinite Earths* 4. July 1985.

Wolfman, Marv. "Crisis on Infinite Comics." In *Crisis on Infinite Earths Companion Deluxe Edition Vol. 1*, edited by Alex Galer. New York: DC Comics, 2018.

Wolfman, Marv. "Introduction." In *Crisis on Infinite Earths*, edited by Rick Taylor and Jim Spivey. New York: DC Comics, 2000.

4 Beyond the Multiverse

Though the imaginary world of DC Comics might feature the most complex and structured multiverse in the annals of world-building, it is by no means the *only* imaginary world to involve a multiverse. Indeed, thanks in no small part to the central role the multiverse has played in DC's cosmology, most other superhero comic book publishers have at least toyed with the idea of a multiverse of their own, especially DC's biggest rival, Marvel Comics. For Marvel, though, consistency has always been more important than multiplicity, and so the multiverse has never quite taken on the same level of importance to Marvel Comics as it has to DC. Tellingly, the translation of Marvel Comics to film and television in recent years has focused on creating a cohesive cinematic universe that links the output of the company's film and television divisions, while DC's adaptations have embraced presenting multiple versions of characters in different media, including bringing the multiverse itself to life.

This chapter will discuss the influence of the DC Multiverse outside the pages of DC Comics. I will begin by looking at how the multiverse has been portrayed in various adaptations of those comics—in novels, animation, and live-action television—and how the conceptualization of the multiverse traverses these different media. Next, I will take a cursory look at the Marvel Multiverse in order to showcase the crucial differences between it and the DC Multiverse, highlighting the unique storytelling priorities of the two companies. Finally, I will examine one particular comic book pastiche of the multiverse concept—Nick Spencer and Christian Ward's *Infinite Vacation*—in order to show how other creators can pick up on the tropes developed by DC Comics in order to build their own imaginary worlds that utilize a multiverse to create emotionally resonant stories.

Novels

In 2006, in the wake of *Infinite Crisis* and the return of the multiverse to DC Comics, Marv Wolfman adopted his own work on *Crisis on Infinite Earths* into a self-contained novel. Without the evocative, detailed imagery of George Pérez to portray the epic grandeur and scope of the multiverse, Wolfman narrowed the scale of his story to tell it mostly from the first-person perspective of Barry Allen as he watches and participates in the events of the story (including story beats from which he was entirely absent in the original comic series).

Distilling a dense, complex, continuity-rich 12-issue storyline into one novel is no easy task, but Wolfman approached it by emphasizing Barry's emotional reactions—or lack thereof—to the destruction of the multiverse. In the preface, Barry introduces the multiverse with a rather neutral tone, summing it up as follows:

> Similarities and differences. Neither better nor worse. Just different. Many Earths, many dimensions, all separate. Nobody knew how this developed, whether by chance or circumstance, but as long as the universes remained separate, nobody needed to worry. And so it went. There was a Multiverse of heroes, some nearly identical to the other, most radically different.
>
> (3)

When the multiverse is finally destroyed, and reborn as the DC Universe, Barry is equally value-neutral, focusing instead on his happiness at the occurrence, and his willingness to surrender to the afterlife (which for speedsters in DC Comics involves merging with the source of their powers, the so-called Speed Force):

> The universe shuddered. And creation began all over again. . . . The universe was reborn. The hows, whys, and wherefores, all T's crossed and all I's dotted, weren't important now. I opened my eyes to find myself in the speed force: colors swirled around me and I felt calm, happy, and ready to pitch my tent permanently here. Couldn't have happened to a more deserving guy.
>
> (310–312)

When Earth-Two's Superman learns that the multiverse has been reborn as a single universe, his reaction is more emotionally raw: "Then there's only one Lois on the Earth. Are you telling me my wife's gone as if she never existed. . . . Except for me, does any of my life still exist? . . . So why am I still here?" (323).

The novelization of *Crisis on Infinite Earths* gave Wolfman an opportunity to take the emphasis away from the epic, multiversal plot of the story and instead look at the way the events of that story affected DC's characters, particularly Barry Allen and the Superman of Earth-Two. The novel gives different shades and colors to the emotional nuances of *Crisis*, skimping on some of the heavy lifting of continuity that was a part of the original comic book in order to tell a more accessible story that focuses on the emotional implications of the loss of the multiverse.

Following the novelization of *Crisis on Infinite Earths*, DC would publish several more novels based on their multiverse-defining *Crisis* stories—*Infinite Crisis, 52, Countdown to Final Crisis* (a yearlong weekly series that served as a kind of prelude to Morrison's series), and *Final Crisis*. Rather than being adapted by the original creators, though, these books were all written by author Greg Cox, who had a long history of crafting media tie-in novels. In adapting the four series, Cox took somewhat less liberty than Wolfman did when recreating his own material. Instead of making massive changes, he focused on trying to distill the complex continuities of the stories into an experience that could be enjoyed (and understood) by an audience unfamiliar with the original comics.

In these novels, Cox is able to overcome one of the few limitations of the original comics—the necessity to visualize every idea, even those that are inherently ineffable. For example, in his adaptation of *Infinite Crisis*, Cox takes the recurring image of the creation of the DC Universe—the cosmic hand made out of stars—and describes it in a way that would be impossible to draw on the comics page:

> [C]reation itself seemed to emerge from some sort of primordial cosmic vortex . . . [which] arose from an open hand the size of a galaxy. Instead of flesh and blood, the celestial hand was composed of the raw materials of time and space.
>
> (103)

Later, when Alexander Luthor recreates the multiverse, Cox is able to kinetically paint the apocalyptic vision that the heroes see in the sky, an image that, in the comic book, is contained within a single, static picture:

> The other two heroes stared up at the chaotic profusion of Earths. . . . [T]hey could see at a glance how volatile the situation was. Duplicate Earths exploded spontaneously before their eyes, coming apart like fabled Krypton itself. Other Earths collided with catastrophic results, while still more hovered ominously in the sky.
>
> (284–285)

Cox brings a similar sense of motion to Booster Gold's vision of the new multiverse being born at the end of the novelization of *52*:

> [D]ays and nights rushed past them at dizzying speed. The sun streaked across the sky, rising and setting every few minutes. Sunlight and starry nights alternated in rapid succession. A waxing moon chased the sun across the celestial firmament. The lights of Metropolis blinked on and off like a message in Morse code. . . . [T]he city's familiar skyline suddenly split apart into dozens of overlapping views of the same scene.
>
> (343)

Although these passages that bring a sense of the ineffable to the DC Multiverse are a nice touch in Cox's prose adaptations, they also serve to underscore the inherently scopophilic nature of the DC Multiverse. The visual cues that differentiate the heroes of multiple Earths must be replaced with prose tags calling them Superman-One, Superman-Two, and so forth, a practice that confusingly interrupts the narrative flow. Similarly, without the powerful drawings of artists such as *Infinite Crisis*'s Phil Jimenez and *Final Crisis*'s J.G. Jones, the scope of the story gets rendered down to the basic movements of the plot, without the background details that are such an important part of this kind of epic storytelling in the comics. It's understandable, then, that prose novels based on superhero comics have never been all that successful,[1] financially or critically, and that the medium has been far more successful in its translations to the visual media of film, television, and animation.

Animation

Since the early *Superman* cartoons produced by Fleischer Studios in the 1940s, there has been a long tradition of adapting DC's heroes to the medium of animation, wherein the superpowered exploits of the characters can be reproduced faithfully without the budgetary concerns of live action. As such, several of these animated adaptations have utilized the multiverse to tell stories about DC characters, since such productions have the ability to portray the epic scope so often demanded of multiverse narratives.

One example of this came in a two-part episode of the *Justice League* animated series, 2002's "Legends," wherein four members of the League are transported to a parallel Earth where they meet the Justice Guild of America, an homage to both the Justice Society and to the Justice League of the 1960s. However, the episode (dedicated to Gardner Fox) ultimately reveals the relatively innocent world of the Justice Guild to be a psychic illusion created by the survivor of a nuclear holocaust. As such, it serves as commentary—much like Geoff Johns' take in *Infinite Crisis*—on the false nature of nostalgia, and the inherent flaw in holding up contemporary narratives to the same moral standards of older narratives that were perhaps not as innocent as they seem on the surface.

Another animated multiverse appeared in the 2010 direct-to-video feature-length film *Justice League: Crisis on Two Earths*. Roughly adapted both from Gardner Fox and Mike Sekowsky's "Crisis on Earth-Three!" storyline and Grant Morrison and Frank Quitely's *JLA: Earth 2* graphic novel, the movie features the heroic Lex Luthor of an Earth run by the Crime Syndicate coming to the Justice League's Earth in order to recruit their help. While the story proves to be rather straightforward, emphasizing action over plot or character, it does take an interesting approach to the multiverse's philosophical impact. The biggest villain of the movie turns out to be Owlman, the Crime Syndicate's version of Batman, who becomes overwhelmed by existential nihilism when he realizes that no choice he ever makes matters, as somewhere in the multiverse another version of him has made a different choice. Unfortunately, this would prove to only be a minor subplot in a vehicle for a relatively simple good-versus-evil story, and the movie as a whole does not make as much use of the multiverse as other versions of the same story have.

Surprisingly, despite the ability of animation to create the visual iconography of the multiverse in a much simpler way than live-action television can, it is in the latter medium that the multiverse has been much more broadly explored.

Live-Action Television

It has only been in recent years that computerized special effects have evolved to a level that has allowed for an adaptation of the DC Multiverse to live-action television. Though some earlier shows such as *Lois & Clark: The New Adventures of Superman* (1993–1997) and *Smallville* (2001–2011) featured the occasional parallel world or alternate timeline, neither ever went so far as to work towards creating a coherent multiverse.[2] It wasn't until the advent of producer Greg Berlanti's "Arrowverse" series of shows that the multiverse became a regular part of DC's television series.

The Arrowverse takes its name from *Arrow*, the first show to premiere in this TV version of the DC Universe, which debuted in 2012. The series stars the Green Arrow, Oliver Queen, a millionaire vigilante who bears as much in common with Batman as he does the comic book hero from which he takes his name. Though *Arrow*, in its first few seasons, focused on semi-realistic vigilantes and villains without any super powers, in the second season the show introduced its version of Barry Allen, who then spun off into his own series, *The Flash*. This show was much more focused on superheroics, with Barry facing off against a series of villains who gained powers from the same accident that gave him his super-speed. At the end of the first season, while attempting to send his arch-nemesis, the Reverse-Flash, back home to the future world from which he came, Barry and his allies open up a wormhole that shoots out a strange, bowl-shaped metal hat. Comic book readers would instantly recognize this lost chapeau as belonging to Jay Garrick, the original Flash.

Season 2 of *The Flash*, following up on this tease, brought the multiverse to the fore. Jay Garrick himself appears in the second episode, fittingly titled "Flash of Two Worlds," to tell Barry and his allies about the multiverse, and about how an evil speedster named Zoom is running free on his own world of Earth-Two. Throughout the remainder of the season, characters would travel back and forth between Barry's Earth-One and Jay's Earth-Two as the heroes attempt to fight back against Zoom. When Barry takes a trip to Earth-Two himself, he meets evil, superpowered versions of his friends Cisco and Caitlin. This encounter would haunt the pair as the series continued, making them wonder about their own potential to turn evil under different circumstances.

Given that the Arrowverse shows focus as much on soap operatics as they do superheroics, by and large they utilize the multiverse in this way to create further internal drama and external melodrama. Alternate versions of heroes don't appear just for a team-up, but also to haunt the shows' protagonists with their own past and potential future decisions. In *Arrow*, for example, the Earth-Two evil version of one dead hero, Laurel Lance, becomes a regular character whose every appearance tortures the "real" Laurel's father. On *The Flash*, Barry encounters another version of Jay Garrick who is his Earth's doppelgänger of Barry's dead father. The multiverse opens up the opportunity for emotional exploration of the series' characters, and to further the ongoing dramatic stakes that are part and parcel of serialized television storytelling.

In addition, the Arrowverse multiverse provides plenty of opportunity for fun and play. In the second season, genius scientist Harry Wells—Earth-Two's version of Dr. Harrison Wells, who had turned out to be the Reverse-Flash in the first season—comes to Earth-One and becomes an ally to Barry. This allowed for actor Tom Cavanagh to remain a series regular, while simultaneously exploring a new character that differed in tone and sensibility from the one he portrayed in the first season. This would continue in the third season, with Cavanagh taking on still *another* version of Wells, "H.R. Wells," this time as something of a comic relief character. Cavanagh seems to revel in the opportunity to play all of these different roles, and the show's writers are thus able to milk the various iterations of Wells for humor as well as pathos.

The writers and producers behind the Arrowverse are also not averse to using the multiverse for epic storytelling every now and again. The various series—which have come to include *Arrow, The Flash, Supergirl,* and the time-traveling team-up show *Legends of Tomorrow*—have an annual crossover, wherein the shows' creators attempt to raise the stakes every year in the same way that the writers and artists of the old JLA/JSA team-ups did. Because *Supergirl* first appeared on CBS before, in its second season, transferring to the CW network (on which all the other shows originated), that series and all of its characters exist on a separate Earth. Thus, every major crossover involves using the multiverse in order to get Supergirl involved in the action.

In the first crossover, 2016's "Invasion!" Barry travels to Supergirl's Earth in order to obtain her help against an alien invasion, with the action then taking place entirely on Earth-One. In 2017, the scope expanded even further. While Supergirl and her sister are visiting Earth-One for Barry's wedding, which is also attended by most of the heroes from the rest of the Arrowverse, the assembled characters are attacked by Nazis from Earth-X, led by evil versions of Supergirl and Green Arrow. The entire story, which took place across all four shows over the course of a week, crosses back and forth between Earth-One and Earth-X, introducing the heroes of the latter planet while simultaneously showing Supergirl and Green Arrow what would happen if they turned away from fighting for good. Perhaps most importantly, much as Len Wein had used the Nazis of Earth-X to comment on the Vietnam War in the 1970s, the Arrowverse writers and producers were clearly using this story—named, after Wein's story, "Crisis on Earth-X!"—to stand in opposition to the resurgence of neo-Nazism in the United States in 2017, and to show the Nazis sorely defeated by the coalition of heroes of various ethnicities and sexual orientations.

The 2018 Arrowverse crossover, "Elseworlds", went even farther than this, bringing in references to *Smallville* and to an earlier Flash live-action series from the 1990s, along with the first live-action version of the Monitor from *Crisis*. In fact, the crossover ended by teasing 2019's crossover a year in advance—the Arrowverse's own version of *Crisis on Infinite Earths*.

"Elseworlds" introduced the idea that perhaps *all* of DC's live-action television shows, and even films, take place within their own multiverse. Geoff Johns, who has written for and produced several of those shows and films, pictures the live action shows as "much like the multiverse in the comics" without any "hard, fast rules saying [they] aren't in the same universe" (quoted in Burlingame). Perhaps, then, there remains the potential for *all* of DC's various multiverses—the DC Multiverse of the comics, the parallel Earths of the animated Justice League stories, and the live-action multiverse of the Arrowverse—to one day link up, in a way that is similar to the omni-connected multiverse of Marvel Comics.

The Marvel Multiverse

Whereas the main line of DC Comics has always followed the central Earth in the multiverse (whether it's known as Earth-One, New Earth, or Earth-Zero), Marvel Comics' primary continuity takes place in a reality with a far less self-important designation—Earth-616. This label is the handiwork of two British creators, writer Alan Moore and artist Alan Davis, in their work on the "Captain Britain" strip published in various titles for the Marvel UK imprint. The pair took the transportation to magical dimensions of earlier Captain Britain stories and turned it into the background for a science-fiction story, revealing the hero to merely be one member of the much larger, interdimensional "Captain Britain Corps." In the seventh issue of the anthology comic *The Daredevils*, Moore and Davis' Captain Britain story offhandedly reveals that the hero is actually "Captain Britain of Earth 616" (136). Moore would later explain in his introduction to a collection of his Captain Britain stories that he chose the number randomly because he was amused by "the parallel-world notion taken to absurd lengths" (8). This label would later be taken up by other Marvel writers, particularly longtime *X-Men* scribe Chris Claremont, and became canon as the name of the Earth on which the vast majority of Marvel's stories take place.

However, as opposed to DC's seeming obsession with creating an organized cosmology for their multiverse, Marvel has always been a bit more laissez-faire when it has come to creating parallel worlds. Starting in 1977, the company has semi-regularly produced ongoing series and one-shot specials under the title *What If?* These stories showcase out-of-continuity alternate realities where certain aspects of the Marvel Universe have unfolded in a different way, such as "What if Spider-Man Had Joined the Fantastic Four?" or "What if Captain America Had Been Elected President?" Many of these stories are presented by a framing sequence featuring the all-seeing being known as The Watcher, who narrates these tales and claims that they come from parallel Earths he has the ability to view. Some of these *What If?* scenarios would later be revisited in the in-continuity team book *Exiles*, which featured heroes able to cross from world to world in the Marvel Multiverse.

As the above examples show, rather than working at a cosmology or a cosmic hierarchy, Marvel's creators have by and large just had fun with their multiverse, utilizing it as an interesting part of the Marvel mythos but by no means giving it the central role that it plays for DC Comics. Since the earliest days of the company's superhero line, when writer Stan Lee and his team of artists (particularly Jack Kirby and Steve Ditko) co-created most of the major heroes, Marvel Comics was obsessed with consistency. Unlike the more slapdash continuity of DC Comics, which has featured several reboots over time, Marvel sees its entire universe as one extended narrative with a sliding timescale to account for its characters' lack of aging. The Marvel Multiverse also maintains that obsession with consistency; because Marvel has never adjusted its line-wide continuity, it has never felt the need to reboot the multiverse in the way that DC has.

The multiverse of Marvel Comics, then, differs from the DC Multiverse. While both explore multiplicity, for Marvel there is no "legacy" aspect to the multiverse. Rather than using the multiverse to bring back older characters, Marvel explores alternate versions of their heroes and characters within the alternate worlds of their multiverse. The Marvel Multiverse is thus much larger than the DC Multiverse, as every alternate Earth or *What If?* scenario becomes just another numbered Earth in the Marvel Multiverse, rather than having to be justified as part of a larger cosmology, as happens at DC. Finally, the biggest Marvel crossover events tend to focus simply on Earth-616, instead of expanding to a multiversal-level threat the way that DC's *Crisis*-level events do.

The two companies' multiverses also vary in terms of how they approach transmedia adaptations of their stories. Whereas the DC Multiverse (at least in its first two phases) consists solely of the worlds found on the printed pages of DC Comics, Marvel's multiverse includes the animated and live-action films and TV series featuring its characters. As comics scholar William Proctor puts it:

> Where Marvel and DC deviate from one another . . . is that the latter utilizes the conceit [of a multiverse] as an intra-medial model for its panoply of comic books, whereas the Marvel multiverse functions as a transmedia firmament encapsulating an entire catalog within its narrative rubric.
>
> (319)

He further explains that:

> Whereas Marvel has created a multiverse that contains within its ambit the entire contents of its various transmedia adventures, DC has repeatedly stressed that its comic book universe and media extensions, such as film and animation series, are separate entities. . . . [R]ather than having live-action material function

as apocrypha or appendages to the comic book universe, Marvel emphatically states that these events take place on Earth-199999, thereby legitimizing the various texts as fully functioning components of the multiverse. Comic book "super-readers" can rationalize film continuity as part of the Marvel multiverse, but non-fans and casual viewers do not need to have extensive knowledge of the Marvel storyworld to visit the cinema and enjoy the latest Marvel film.

(337–340)

Thus, for Marvel, the multiverse is a corporate tool as much as it is a narrative tool, allowing the company to link its disparate continuities—from the comics, the movies, the television shows, and so forth—into one overarching superstructure. While DC Comics has worked harder to define the parameters of its multiverse than Marvel Comics has and has used it to create a richer tapestry of narratives, Marvel has taken the idea beyond the realm of narrative to show how a multiverse can be useful not just to an imaginary world, but to the profit margin of the owner(s) of that world.

Infinite Vacation

Given how the multiverses of the two largest comic book companies have been used as a money-making tool at least as often as they've been used to tell creative, engaging stories, it's no surprise that the concept has come up for parody, pastiche, and play in the works of comics produced by other publishers. The series that takes this to its biggest extreme thus far is Nick Spenser and Christian Ward's four-issue miniseries *Infinite Vacation*, published by Image Comics.

The premise of *Infinite Vacation* is summed up early on in the first issue, in the form of a commercial for the titular service:

With the Infinite Vacation's patented transuniversal displacement technology, now you can trade, buy, and sell your way through a marketplace made up of limitless numbers of alternate reality iterations of yourself. Not limited to merely one or two way trades,

> our peer-to-peer instant auction digital commerce engine can coordinate quadrillions of life change transactions each second—creating an intricate and highly mobile network of possibilities that surpass the scale of human imagination. You just download our free app, available on most mobile devices, and set up your user profile—then search for the life change you want, and choose from a detailed list of available opportunities—all put up for purchase by other yous. Everything from the most trivial, slight difference in your life, to the most grandiose, completely divergent path—it's all at your fingertips now.
>
> (7)

The series follows one such vacationer, named Mark, who has become addicted to the process, and finds himself ceaselessly changing realities, exchanging lives with different versions of himself but always ending up unhappy. Shortly into the first issue, one such alternate version tells him why he thinks this is:

> You got yourself so hooked on . . . how you can "have anything—live everything." . . . [Y]ou're so obsessed with having *everything*, you can't enjoy *anything*. My advice? Just find *one* thing, dude. Find that *one* thing that makes your life worth more than you can put up for sale on your phone, and give that everything you got. You hearin' me?
>
> (12)

From its outset, *Infinite Vacation* wears its metaphor on its sleeve. When, only a few pages later, Mark meets a mysterious girl named Claire, Spencer and Ward telegraph that she will be the "one thing" he comes to care about. The cross-reality science-fiction action-adventure that follows—with other versions of Mark from across the universes turning up dead one by one—is all in service to this romantic subplot, leading up to Mark ultimately deciding, in the fourth issue, to stay in one reality, "A world with her in it" (59). Despite the infinite possibilities of death-defying adventure posed by the multiverse, Spencer and

Ward argue that the true adventure, love, can only flourish by finding that one thing that's most important to you and never letting it go.

The DC Multiverse, of course, can't be reduced down to a simple metaphor in the way the multiverse created by Spencer and Ward can. However, the creators' larger point is still resonant here on a broader level. Despite an attempt to restructure DC Comics' imaginary world into a singular, coherent universe, fans and creators still remembered the multiverse as a part of that world's inherent charm. It was, in some ways, the "one thing" that made DC stand out from the more stream-lined continuity of Marvel. As we have seen, these fans never let go of the idea of the DC Multiverse, and eventually it came back in full force. Its tangled history shows us not only that an audience's love for something has the potential to bring it back, but also teaches us the various roles that a multiverse can play in building and maintaining an imaginary world.

Notes

1 Perhaps the most successful line of superhero novels is the "shared world" *Wild Cards* line, written by a multitude of different writers and edited/over-seen by George R.R. Martin. These books featured characters and stories designed for the prose medium and were able to approach heavily adult material long before comics publishers were willing to let creators do the same with their superheroes.

2 When *Smallville*'s story was continued after the series finale as a comic book, however, the main storyline turned its focus to the multiverse, leading up to its own version of *Crisis*. What had been impossible to achieve visu-ally on television, at least within a reasonable budget, was relatively normal fare for comic books.

References

Burlingame, Russ. "Geoff Johns Teases Multiverse with DC Universe Shows." *Comic Book.* Last modified October 3, 2018. www.comicbook.com/dc/2018/10/04/geoff-johns-teases-multiverse-with-dc-universe-shows/.

Cox, Greg. *Infinite Crisis*. New York: Ace Books, 2005.

Cox, Greg. *52*. New York: Ace Books, 2007.

Moore, Alan. "Introduction." In *Captain Britain Omnibus*, edited by Mark D. Beazley. New York: Marvel Comics, 2009.

Moore, Alan, writer, Alan Davis, artist, et al. "Rough Justice," *The Daredevils* 7. Reprinted in *Captain Britain Omnibus*, edited by Mark D. Beazley. New York: Marvel Comics, 2009.

Proctor, William. "Schrödinger's Cape: The Quantum Seriality of the Marvel Universe." In *Make Ours Marvel: Media Convergence and a Comics Universe*, edited by Matt Yockey. Austin, TX: University of Texas Press, 2017.

Spencer, Nick, scripter, Christian Ward, artist, et al. *Infinite Vacation* 1. Reprinted in *Infinite Vacation*, edited by Jane Dodge. Berkeley, CA: Image Comics, 2013.

Spencer, Nick, scripter, Christian Ward, artist, et al. *Infinite Vacation* 4. Reprinted in *Infinite Vacation*, edited by Jane Dodge. Berkeley, CA: Image Comics, 2013.

Wolfman, Marv. *Crisis on Infinite Earths*. New York: ibooks, 2005.

Conclusion

The writers, artists, editors, and other creators working for DC Comics did not originate the idea of a multiverse, nor were they the first people to utilize the trope of alternate worlds in order to explore more deeply the nature of their characters. What makes the DC Multiverse stand out is the ways in which it is so intimately connected to the entire structure of DC Comics' imaginary world, and the intricate cosmology that its creators have established over its more than half a century of existence. The meticulous detail with which various writers and artists have built and charted the DC Multiverse rivals any other imaginary world as far as sheer scope and scale, making it the preeminent example of how a multiverse can be a vital element to any fictional worldscape.

For anybody interested in better understanding imaginary worlds, whether for scholarly purposes, personal interest, or a desire to create imaginary worlds of one's own, the DC Multiverse thus provides several takeaways as to how such worlds can benefit from a multiverse to tell resonant stories and create a deeper and more intense sense of completeness and immersion for audiences. I have broken this down into four key ways in which a multiverse aids subcreators in building imaginary worlds, based on the four themes of the DC Multiverse we have seen reiterated over and over again: legacy, multiplicity, expansion, and play.

Legacy

To review the history of the DC Multiverse is to review the history of DC Comics as a publishing entity. The creation and development of the multiverse takes in the earliest superhero stories of the so-called "Golden Age," the return of heroes in the "Silver Age," the more serious, "mature" reinventions of the 1970s–1990s, and finally the transmedia popularity of superheroes in the twenty-first century. Throughout that entire history, the multiverse is constantly "bringing back" something that has been lost or forgotten in DC Comics, whether that is the reappearance of the Justice Society in the 1960s or the resurgence of specific parallel worlds at the end of *52*.

The DC Multiverse has helped to solidify the sense of legacy that lies at the heart of the DC Comics imaginary world. While Marvel may eclipse DC in terms of popularity, or even creativity, it doesn't have any characters as long-lasting as the classic heroic archetypes embodied by Superman, Batman, and Wonder Woman. The characters published by DC Comics are the original superheroes, and the publisher has never gone through a period where it wasn't producing the ongoing adventures of at least those three heroes. This legacy of superheroics is what makes DC distinctive as a comic book publisher, and the company has utilized the multiverse time and again to cement that legacy and bring back reminders of the company's vast history.

By allowing subcreators to create multiple versions of the same character, a multiverse can maintain an imaginary world's legacy by helping its characters to remain ageless. As Mark J.P. Wolf notes, "Genealogies function as extensions of character, which in turn provide continuity across a world's eras. . . . Yet as a world grows temporally, it often passes beyond the lifespan of individual characters" (170). In a multiverse, however, subcreators need not necessarily face that problem, as they can bring in an alternate version of the same character.

Thus, alongside the notion of legacy, a multiverse can also bring about renewal. A fresh version of the imaginary world can be created as an alternate world in the same multiverse, with subtle differences. This is what DC Comics did after *Crisis*, after all, and then several decades later they brought back the multiverse, turning once again to the heroic legacy of its oldest characters. A multiverse can help subcreators focus on core concepts of character, and to recreate, renew, and remember crucial aspects of their imaginary world as needed.

Multiplicity

Perhaps the most obvious lesson of the DC Multiverse is that readers and audiences do not have a problem encountering multiple versions of the same character. They can differentiate between the young, single Superman of Earth-One and the older, married Superman of Earth-Two, and appreciate the differences between the two versions of the character and the kinds of stories that creators can tell with them. Indeed, some of the most critically acclaimed and commercially popular stories from DC Comics—such as Frank Miller's *The Dark Knight Returns* (1986), Alan Moore and Curt Swan's *Whatever Happened to the Man of Tomorrow?* (1986), and Grant Morrison and Frank Quitely's *All-Star Superman* (2005–2008)—have taken place outside of the main continuity, and even outside of the general cosmology of the multiverse.

Despite what Marv Wolfman and the rest of DC's editorial and executive team may have felt at the outset of *Crisis on Infinite Earths*, a great many readers *prefer* an imaginary world where there are multiple versions of the same character. Presenting more than one iteration of a character, and having those different versions interact with one another, can not only create a powerful narrative, but also, through contrasts, reveal more about the inherent nature of that character. What better way to see just how much Superman values human life than by contrasting him to a Superman who kills?

The multiplicity that comes as an inherent part of a multiverse is thus a tool of both narrative and character. Subcreators can develop a panoply of stories revolving around multiple versions of the same character, and all the while can reveal ever-more layers of the original/"real" version of that character. Thus, by presenting points of variation, a multiverse can be used to reify the central conceits and concerns of a given imaginary world. As Henry Jenkins argues:

> Multiplicity seems to exist with continuity at the present moment: fans are expected to know which interpretive frame should be applied to any given title. . . . [M]any of these stories reaffirm the underlying logic to these characters. Batman would have behaved

more or less the same in another time and place. Superman and Lex Luthor were destined to be archrivals. The more we change, the more it is clear that the world depicted in the normal continuity had to be what it is because of the core integrity of these characters.

(307–308)

Ironically, multiplicity helps subcreators reveal the singular nature of their imaginary worlds by reiterating and solidifying core concepts, as well as expanding upon those concepts.

Expansion

On a commercial level, the multiverse has proven most useful to DC Comics by allowing the publisher to add on a variety of intellectual properties as a part of the same imaginary world, particularly whenever DC has purchased the intellectual property of other comic book publishers and chosen to integrate them into the multiverse (such as the Quality Comics heroes who would populate Earth-X, or more recently the heroes from Wildstorm Comics). These types of additions to the multiverse are, as Wolf puts it, "retroactive linkages" forming "the connections between two worlds which were conceived and made separately, and not originally intended to be connected" (216).

These types of retroactive linkages aren't limited to corporate purchases and mergers, but can be a part of any creator's individual imaginary world-building. Indeed, as Wolf notes, "Retroactive linkages are most commonly found in the work of authors who have created two or more imaginary worlds and wish to bring them together into one larger creation" (216). Often such an author:

desires to consolidate his or her efforts into one larger, overarching world. . . . While retroactive linkages can be done for artistic reasons . . . it may also be done for commercial reasons. . . . Whatever the case, retroactive linkages can alter the context and canonicity of a work, and change how an audience sees a particular world and the overarching narratives taking place within it.

(218)

These retroactive linkages—which I call, more simply, "expansions"—are easily implemented when an imaginary world is structured around (or at least considered a part of) a multiverse. Though this expansion may, as Wolf explains, change the context of a work or world, that can be the point of such an exercise. For example, the violent, extreme characters of Wildstorm, created during the "grim and gritty" period of superhero comics in the 1990s, become vastly different when contextualized as a part of the DC Multiverse, with its legacy of classic heroes.

A multiverse thus provides an imaginary world with the potential to make additions to its canon and to expand beyond whatever its current boundaries are, giving creators more room to build and more room to play.

Play

The final key feature of the DC Multiverse is also, in many ways, the most important—it's just plain fun. The epic scope of stories enabled by the multiverse, and wide range of characters starring in these stories, are richly imaginative, sometimes deeply moving, and always energized by a sense of play on the part of both the readers and creators. The bigger the creative toy box, the more fun that everybody involved is able to have, and the DC Multiverse has one of the biggest toy boxes of them all. According to Wolf:

> Subcreation is not just a desire, but a need and a right; it renews our vision and gives us new perspective and insight into ontological questions that might otherwise escape our notice within the default assumptions we make about reality. Subcreated worlds also direct our attention beyond themselves, moving us beyond the quotidian and the material, increasing our awareness of how we conceptualize, understand, and imagine the Primary World.
>
> (287)

DC Comics achieves these goals by developing not just one subcreated world, but a whole multiverse of worlds, of varying degree of similarity, that use the tropes of superhero narratives to create mythic, melodramatic stories of good versus evil, where good always triumphs in the end.

The epic scope of these stories, Jenkins argues, prefigures many contemporary imaginary worlds: "The superhero genre anticipates the focus on expansive and immersive story worlds" (304). The immersive world of the DC Multiverse, and the expansive scale of the stories therein, are thus vital parts of DC's massive subcreation, through which various creators are able to raise various ontological questions.

The way that the DC Multiverse has sustained such questioning over such a long period of time, though, is that these probing examinations are always couched in highly entertaining superhero stories. As expansive as the DC Multiverse gets, it is at its core an imaginary world of superheroes, a genre that is meant to inspire, energize, and entertain. Without this entertainment, without the inherent sense of play at the core of the DC Multiverse, and of DC Comics in general, then all the rest of the imaginary world gets lost.

Creators and readers return to the world of DC Comics not just because of its multiverse, but because as a company it is adept at telling engaging, entertaining superhero stories. The fact that these stories are set in a multiverse only makes them, for many readers, more entertaining, creating a deeper level of engagement for the avid fan who enjoys understanding the broader cosmology of the imaginary world. The multiverse creates a more inventive, complete, and consistent imaginary world for DC Comics, developing an endless vista of stories with innumerable permutations of characters.

There are, in the end, as many potential avenues of exploration and creativity that the imaginary world of DC Comics can take as there are infinite worlds in the multiverse.

References

Jenkins, Henry. "Managing Multiplicity in Superhero Comics." In *Third Person: Authoring and Exploring Vast Narratives*, edited by Pat Harrigan and Noah Wardrip-Fruin. Cambridge, MA: MIT Press, 2009.

Wolf, Mark J.P. *Building Imaginary Worlds: The Theory and History of Subcreation*. New York: Routledge, 2012.

Index